Sounds & Silences was first published in 1970, twenty years ago, and was welcomed by readers, reviewers, and teachers alike. Over one hundred contemporary poems collected here speak directly to young people today, as they did when they were first published, because they reflect timeless concerns, expressed in modern language. The song lyrics included are a form of expression that is particularly cherished by young people and add to the richness of this unique collection. The themes of the poetry center on topics familiar to readers of all ages: Family, Childhood, Isolation, Identity, Realities, Illusion, Dissent, Communication, Love, War, Pain, and Recollections.

RICHARD PECK is one of the most highly acclaimed and popular writers of fiction for young adults. His many award-winning novels include *Are You in the House Alone?*, *Dreamland Lake*, *Close Enough to Touch*, *Representing Super Doll*, *Secrets of the Shopping Mall*, *Through a Brief Darkness*, *Father Figure*, *Remembering the Good Times*, *Princess Ashley*, and *Those Summer Girls I Never Met*. These are available in Laurel-Leaf editions, as are his anthologies, *Mindscapes* and *Edge of Awareness*. His most recent novel for Delacorte Press, *Voices After Midnight*, will soon be available in a Yearling paperback edition, along with the Blossom Culp books: *The Ghost Belonged to Me*, *Ghosts I Have Been*, *The Dreadful Future of Blossom Culp*, and *Blossom Culp and the Sleep of Death*.

Mr. Peck lives in New York City.

ALSO AVAILABLE IN LAUREL-LEAF BOOKS:

SOUNDS AND SILENCES

POETRY FOR NOW

Edited by *Richard Peck*

Published by
Dell Publishing
a division of
Bantam Doubleday Dell Publishing Group, Inc.
666 Fifth Avenue
New York, New York 10103

To My Mother and Father

*I am grateful to Mrs. Harriet Aufses, librarian of Hunter College High School,
New York City, and to Mr. Curtis Crotty of the English Department of
Evanston Township High School, Evanston, Illinois, for their great help and
encouragement in the compiling of this collection.*

Acknowledgments for copyrighted material appear on pages 158
through 166 and constitute an extension of this page.

ISBN: 0-440-98171-9

Reprinted by arrangement with Delacorte Press

Printed in the United States of America

February 1990

10 9 8 7 6 5 4 3 2 1

KRI

CONTENTS

Introduction   XI

THE FAMILY   1

Little Brand New Baby, TOM PAXTON   2
The Name, ROBERT CREELEY   3
Taught Me Purple, EVELYN TOOLEY HUNT   5
Mother to Son, LANGSTON HUGHES   6
That Dark Other Mountain, ROBERT FRANCIS   7
The Geese, RICHARD PECK   8
What Shall He Tell That Son?,
   CARL SANDBURG   9
My Papa's Waltz, THEODORE ROETHKE   11
The Empty Woman, GWENDOLYN BROOKS   12
Stark Boughs on the Family Tree,
   MARY OLIVER   13
Home Burial, ROBERT FROST   14

CHILDHOOD   19

Declaration of Independence, WOLCOTT GIBBS   20
Drawing by Ronnie C., Grade One,
   RUTH LECHLITNER   21
My Parents Kept Me from Children Who
   Were Rough, STEPHEN SPENDER   22
Boy at the Window, RICHARD WILBUR   23
The Ballad of the Light-Eyed Little Girl,
   GWENDOLYN BROOKS   24

The Ballad of Chocolate Mabbie,
    GWENDOLYN BROOKS   26
Janet Waking, JOHN CROWE RANSOM   27
Prayer Before Birth, LOUIS MAC NEICE   29

ISOLATION   31

Portrait of a Girl with Comic Book,
    PHYLLIS MC GINLEY   32
Fifteen, WILLIAM STAFFORD   33
The Dreamer, WILLIAM CHILDRESS   34
The Cave, GLENN W. DRESBACH   35
Preface to a Twenty Volume Suicide Note,
    LEROI JONES   36
Pastoral, WILLIAM CARLOS WILLIAMS   37

IDENTITY   39

Kennedy, MOLLY KAZAN   40
Yet Do I Marvel, COUNTEE CULLEN   41
The Negro Speaks of Rivers,
    LANGSTON HUGHES   42
Powwow, W. D. SNODGRASS   43
Florida Road Workers, LANGSTON HUGHES 45
Pastures of Plenty, WOODY GUTHRIE   46
Caliban in the Coal Mines, LOUIS UNTERMEYER 47
Sunday Afternoon, DENISE LEVERTOV   48
Two Voices in a Meadow, RICHARD WILBUR 49
Gone Away, DENISE LEVERTOV   50
The Rebel, MARI E. EVANS   51

REALITIES   53

Bendix, JOHN UPDIKE   54
At Breakfast, MAY SWENSON   55
Sonic Boom, JOHN UPDIKE   57
Ice Cream, JONATHAN PRICE   58

The Bat, THEODORE ROETHKE 59

For a Lamb, RICHARD EBERHART 60

Summer: West Side, JOHN UPDIKE 61

Auto Wreck, KARL SHAPIRO 63

The Yachts, WILLIAM CARLOS WILLIAMS 65

Crystal Moment, ROBERT P. TRISTRAM COFFIN 67

Traveling Through the Dark,
    WILLIAM STAFFORD 69

ILLUSION 71

Number 20, LAWRENCE FERLINGHETTI 72

Ego, PHILIP BOOTH 73

Lucy in the Sky with Diamonds, THE BEATLES 74

Museums, LOUIS MAC NEICE 75

Suburban Madrigal, JOHN UPDIKE 76

Sand Hill Road, MORTON GROSSER 77

The Big Rock Candy Mountains, ANONYMOUS 78

The Lifeguard, JAMES DICKEY 80

DISSENT 83

Sketch from Loss of Memory, SONYA DORMAN 84

She's Leaving Home, THE BEATLES 85

Southbound on the Freeway, MAY SWENSON 87

Little Boxes, MALVINA REYNOLDS 89

Target, R. P. LISTER 91

"next to of course god america i,
    e. e. cummings 92

Vapor Trail Reflected in the Frog Pond,
    GALWAY KINNELL 93

The Body Politic, DONALD HALL 95

pity this busy monster, manunkind,
    e. e. cummings 96

The Unknown Citizen, W. H. AUDEN 97

The Angry Man, PHYLLIS MC GINLEY 99

COMMUNICATION 101

Siren Song, MARGARET ATWOOD 102
Thoughts While Driving Home, JOHN UPDIKE 104
Confession Overheard in a Subway,
    KENNETH FEARING 105
An Echo: Sonnet to an Empty Page,
    ROBERT PACK 107
Loneliness, BROOKS JENKINS 108
How She Resolved to Act, MERRILL MOORE 109
A Ritual to Read to Each Other,
    WILLIAM STAFFORD 110
Grandmother, Rocking, EVE MERRIAM 111

LOVE 113

For Anne, LEONARD COHEN 114
Song, LEONARD COHEN 114
To Be in Love, GWENDOLYN BROOKS 115
Sonnet, COUNTEE CULLEN 117
Places, Loved Ones, PHILIP LARKIN 118
somewhere i have never travelled,
    e. e. cummings 119
For Hettie, LEROI JONES 120
The River-Merchant's Wife: A Letter, RIHAKU 121
To D—, Dead by Her Own Hand,
    HOWARD NEMEROV 123

WAR 125

The Sonnet-Ballad, GWENDOLYN BROOKS 126
Where Have All the Flowers Gone?,
    PETE SEEGER 127
Naming of Parts, HENRY REED 129
Of Bombs and Boys, RICHARD CORBIN 131
my sweet old etcetera, e. e. cummings 132

The Death of the Ball Turret Gunner,
    RANDALL JARRELL   134
An Irish Airman Foresees His Death,
    WILLIAM BUTLER YEATS   134
Ultima Ratio Regum, STEPHEN SPENDER   135
The Conscientious Objector, KARL SHAPIRO   136
I've Got to Know, WOODY GUTHRIE   138

PAIN   139

The Heroes, LOUIS SIMPSON   140
Surgical Ward, W. H. AUDEN   141
Hunchback Girl: She Thinks of Heaven,
    GWENDOLYN BROOKS   142
Dark Girl, ARNA BONTEMPS   143
It's Here In The, RUSSELL ATKINS   144
Hurt Hawks, ROBINSON JEFFERS   145

RECOLLECTIONS   147

Sonnet to My Mother, GEORGE BARKER   148
Number 7, LAWRENCE FERLINGHETTI   149
Aunt Helen, T. S. ELIOT   151
Bells for John Whiteside's Daughter,
    JOHN CROWE RANSOM   152
Elegy for Jane, THEODORE ROETHKE   153
The Elementary Scene, RANDALL JARRELL 154
Fern Hill, DYLAN THOMAS   155

Acknowledgments   158
Index of First Lines   167
Index of Authors and Titles   171

INTRODUCTION

Just the other day I was writing a story, a short one called "I Go Along"* about a high-school boy in a small town somewhere. He's in the "slow-learners" English class because his friends are there and because it's an easy life. Then one night for some reason he can't explain to himself, he goes to a poetry reading, even though everybody else in the audience is from the "gifted" program. When the poet comes on the stage, the boy's surprised to find that he isn't dressed like a poet. In fact, he's dressed like the boy: Levi's, big belt, boots.

I wrote the poems the poet reads at the meeting, or rather I ghost-wrote them in the character's voice. One was about his wife. The other was his recollection of being in high school. The boy thinks the first poem is too personal and the second one is too true. He expects them to rhyme too, and they don't.

And oh yes, he meets a girl that night. They go to the same school, but she's in the "gifted" program, so they've never met. They've been living in the little boxes that life puts us in. Does the boy break out that night? Does he begin to change and grow because of a poet's words and a girl he never dreamed he'd know? I leave that for the readers to decide. Both poetry and

* from *Connections, Short Stories by Outstanding Writers for Young Adults*, edited by Donald R. Gallo, Delacorte Press, © 1989.

prose leave a lot up to the readers. It's television that tells you everything it wants you to know.

What has this to do with the poetry and the song lyrics in this collection, *Sounds & Silences*? Only that it's always good to see the effect that poetry and people have on each other. In almost all my novels and stories, I include poetry. Sometimes I borrow from better poets. Sometimes I write the poetry to help close the gap between the characters on the page and the reader holding the book. Whatever you do for a living, poetry comes in handy because it's a shortcut to the truth.

We need both prose and poetry to express who we are, and poetry—quick and surprising—crosses borders in an age when we keep our borders too heavily defended and live too snugly in our little boxes, especially if we're young. You can study poetry, of course, but the interesting thing is, poetry studies you.

I hope you find glimpses of yourself in these poems, and a few long looks too. The selections fall into a pattern familiar to us all: *The Family:* its members and relationships. *Childhood:* when we begin to move from the people who gave us life to lives of our own. *Isolation:* where we begin to confront our most private selves. *Identity:* the quest for achieving that self. *Realities:* the unavoidable and concrete aspects of our world. *Illusion:* the unreal that conflicts with the real. *Dissent:* that growing problem in a conforming world. *Communication:* the need for reaching out. *Love:* the timeless topic that depends upon communication. *War:* the threat to every human impulse. *Pain:* war's companion. And finally, *Recollections:* a second look at things that linger in the mind.

No poet—nobody has the final word on any of these subjects, but that's all right. There's more poetry where this came from, and more to be written by people like you and me. Poetry points out that we aren't as alone as we thought we were, and we'll always need to know that.

RICHARD PECK
New York

THE FAMILY

LITTLE BRAND NEW BABY

Hey, Little Brand New Baby,
Your Momma and your Daddy think you're mighty
  nice.
Hey, Little Brand New Baby,
I hope you have a mighty nice life.

Your Daddy's lookin' mighty proud,
Handin' out cigars all around the town,
grinnin' like a 'Possum
And I think he's gonna crow,
And I hope you have a mighty nice life.

Your Momma waited quite awhile,
Carried you around for half a million miles,
But you know it was worth it when you look at her
  smile,
And I hope you have a mighty nice life.

It all lies ahead of you and from this day
It won't be easy as you travel your way,
But here's to your birth and I just want to say
That I hope you have a mighty nice life.

TOM PAXTON

THE NAME

Be natural,
wise
as you can be,
my daughter,

let my name
be in you flesh
I gave you
in the act of

loving your mother,
all your days
her ways,
the woman in you

brought from
sensuality's measure,
no other,
there was no thought

of it but such
pleasure all women
must be in her,
as you. But not wiser,

not more of nature
than her hair,
the eyes
she gives you.

There will not be another
woman such as you

are. Remember
your mother,

the way you came,
the days of waiting.
Be natural,
daughter, wise

as you can be,
all my daughters,
be women
for men

when that time comes.
Let the rhetoric
stay with me
your father. Let

me talk about it,
saving you such
vicious self-
exposure, let you

pass it on
in you. I cannot
be more than the man
who watches.

ROBERT CREELEY

TAUGHT ME PURPLE

My mother taught me purple
Although she never wore it.
Wash-gray was her circle,
The tenement her orbit.

My mother taught me golden
And held me up to see it,
Above the broken molding,
Beyond the filthy street.

My mother reached for beauty
And for its lack she died,
Who knew so much of duty
She could not teach me pride.

EVELYN TOOLEY HUNT

MOTHER TO SON

Well, Son, I'll tell you
Life for me ain't been no crystal stair
It's had tacks in it,
And splinters,
And boards torn up,
And places with no carpets on the floor,

Bare.
But all the time
I'se been climbin' on
And reachin' landin's
And turning corners
And sometimes goin' on in the dark
Where there ain't been no light.
So, Boy, don't you turn back.
Don't you set down on the steps
'Cause you find it's kinder hard.
Don't you fall now—
For I'se still goin', Honey,
I'se still climbin'
And life for me ain't been
                no crystal stair.

                    LANGSTON HUGHES

THAT DARK OTHER MOUNTAIN

My father could go down a mountain faster than I
Though I was first one up.
Legs braced or with quick steps he slid the gravel
    slopes
Where I picked cautious footholds.

Black, Iron, Eagle, Doublehead, Chocorua,
Wildcat and Carter Dome—
He beat me down them all. And that last other
    mountain,
And that dark other mountain.

ROBERT FRANCIS

THE GEESE

My father was the first to hear
The passage of the geese each fall,
Passing above the house so near
He'd hear within his heart their call.

And then at breakfast time he'd say:
"The geese were heading south last night,"
For he had lain awake till day,
Feeling his earthbound soul take flight.

Knowing that winter's wind comes soon
After the rushing of those wings,
Seeing them pass before the moon,
Recalling the lure of faroff things.

RICHARD PECK

WHAT SHALL HE TELL THAT SON?

A father sees a son nearing manhood.
What shall he tell that son?
"Life is hard; be steel; be a rock."
And this might stand him for the storms
   and serve him for humdrum and monotony
   and guide him amid sudden betrayals
   and tighten him for slack moments.
"Life is soft loam; be gentle; go easy."
And this too might serve him.
Brutes have been gentled where lashes failed.
The growth of a frail flower in a path up
  has sometimes shattered and split a rock.
A tough will counts. So does desire.
So does a rich soft wanting.
Without rich wanting nothing arrives.
Tell him too much money has killed men
   and left them dead years before burial:
   and quest of lucre beyond a few easy needs
   has twisted good enough men
   sometimes into dry thwarted worms.
Tell him time as a stuff can be wasted.
Tell him to be a fool every so often
   and to have no shame over having been a fool
   yet learning something out of every folly
   hoping to repeat none of the cheap follies
   thus arriving at intimate understanding
   of a world numbering many fools
Tell him to be alone often and get at himself
   and above all tell himself no lies about himself,
   whatever the white lies and protective fronts
   he may use amongst other people.

Tell him solitude is creative if he is strong and the
final decisions are made in silent rooms.
Tell him to be different from other people if it
comes natural and easy being different.
Let him have lazy days seeking his deeper motives.
Let him seek deep for where he is a born natural.
   Then he may understand Shakespeare
   and the Wright brothers, Pasteur, Pavlov,
   Michael Faraday and free imaginations bringing
changes into a world resenting change.
   He will be lonely enough
   to have time for the work
   he knows as his own.

CARL SANDBURG

MY PAPA'S WALTZ

The whiskey on your breath
Could make a small boy dizzy;
But I hung on like death:
Such waltzing was not easy.

We romped until the pans
Slid from the kitchen shelf;
My mother's countenance
Could not unfrown itself.

The hand that held my wrist
Was battered on one knuckle;
At every step you missed
My right ear scraped a buckle.

You beat time on my head
With a palm caked hard by dirt,
Then waltzed me off to bed
Still clinging to your shirt.

THEODORE ROETHKE

THE EMPTY WOMAN

The empty woman took toys!
  In her sisters' homes
Were little girls and boys.

The empty woman had hats
To show. With feathers. Wore combs
In polished waves. Wooed cats

And pigeons. Shopped.
Shopped hard for nephew-toys,
Niece-toys. Made taffy. Popped

Popcorn and hated her sisters,
Featherless and waveless but able to
Mend measles, nag noses, blast blisters

And all day waste wordful girls
And war-boys, and all day
Say "Oh God!"—and tire among curls

And plump legs and proud muscle
And blackened school-bags, babushkas, torn socks,
And bouffants that bustle, and rustle.

GWENDOLYN BROOKS

STARK BOUGHS ON THE FAMILY TREE

Up in the attic on row on row,
In dusty frames, with stubborn eyes,
My thin ancestors slowly fade
Under the flat Ohio skies.

And so, I think, they always were:
Like their own portrait, years ago,
They paced the blue and windy fields,
Aged in the polished rooms below.

For name by name I find no sign
Of hero in this distant life,
But only men as calm as snow
Who took some faithful girl as wife,

Who labored while the drought, the flood
Crisscrossed the fickle summer air,
Who built great barns and propped their lives
Upon a slow heart-breaking care.

Why do I love them as I do,
Who dared no glory, won no fame?
In a harsh land that lies subdued,
They are the good boughs of my name.

If music sailed their dreams at all,
They were not heroes, and slept on;
As one by one they left the small
Accomplished, till the great was done.

MARY OLIVER

He saw her from the bottom of the stairs
Before she saw him. She was starting down,
Looking back over her shoulder at some fear.
She took a doubtful step and then undid it
To raise herself and look again. He spoke
Advancing toward her: "What is it you see
From up there always—for I want to know."
She turned and sank upon her skirts at that,
And her face changed from terrified to dull.
He said to gain time: "What is it you see,"
Mounting until she cowered under him.
"I will find out now—you must tell me, dear."
She, in her place, refused him any help
With the least stiffening of her neck and silence.
She let him look, sure that he wouldn't see.
Blind creature; and a while he didn't see.
But at last he murmured, "Oh," and again, "Oh."

"What is it—what?" she said.

                            "Just that I see."

"You don't," she challenged. "Tell me what it is."

"The wonder is I didn't see at once.
I never noticed it from here before.
I must be wonted to it—that's the reason.
The little graveyard where my people are!
So small the window frames the whole of it.
Not so much larger than a bedroom, is it?
There are three stones of slate and one of marble,

Broad-shouldered little slabs there in the sunlight
On the sidehill. We haven't to mind *those*.
But I understand: it is not the stones,
But the child's mound—"

                    "Don't, don't, don't, don't," she cried.

She withdrew shrinking from beneath his arm
That rested on the banister, and slid downstairs;
And turned on him with a daunting look,
He said twice over before he knew himself:
"Can't a man speak of his own child he's lost?"

"Not you! Oh, where's my hat? Oh, I don't need it!
I must get out of here. I must get air.
I don't know rightly whether any man can."

"Amy! Don't go to someone else this time.
Listen to me. I won't come down the stairs."
He sat and fixed his chin between his fists.
"There's something I should like to ask you, dear."

"You don't know how to ask it."

                              "Help me, then."

Her fingers moved the latch for all reply.

"My words are nearly always an offense.
I don't know how to speak of anything
So as to please you. But I might be taught
I should suppose. I can't say I see how.
A man must partly give up being a man

With women-folk. We could have some arrange-
    ment
By which I'd bind myself to keep hands off
Anything special you're a-mind to name.
Though I don't like such things 'twixt those that
    love.
Two that don't love can't live together without
    them.
But two that do can't live together with them."
She moved the latch a little. "Don't—don't go.
Don't carry it to someone else this time.
Tell me about it if it's something human.
Let me into your grief. I'm not so much
Unlike other folks as your standing there
Apart would make me out. Give me my chance.
I do think, though, you overdo it a little.
What was it brought you up to think it the thing
To take your mother-loss of a first child
So inconsolably—in the face of love.
You'd think his memory might be satisfied—"

"There you go sneering now!"

                        "I'm not, I'm not!

You make me angry. I'll come down to you.
God, what a woman! And it's come to this,
A man can't speak of his own child that's dead."

"You can't because you don't know how to speak.
If you had any feelings, you that dug
With your own hand—how could you?—his little
    grave;
I saw you from that very window there,

Making the gravel leap and leap in air,
Leap up, like that, like that, and land so lightly
And roll back down the mound beside the hole.
I thought, Who is that man? I didn't know you.
And I crept down the stairs and up the stairs
To look again, and still your spade kept lifting.
Then you came in. I heard your rumbling voice
Out in the kitchen, and I don't know why,
But I went near to see with my own eyes.
You could sit there with the stains on your shoes
Of the fresh earth from your own baby's grave
And talk about your everyday concerns.
You had stood the spade up against the wall
Outside there in the entry, for I saw it."

"I shall laugh the worst laugh I ever laughed.
I'm cursed. God, if I don't believe I'm cursed."

"I can repeat the very words you were saying.
'Three foggy mornings and one rainy day
Will rot the best birch fence a man can build.'
Think of it, talk like that at such a time!
What had how long it takes a birch to rot
To do with what was in the darkened parlor.
You *couldn't* care! The nearest friends can go
With anyone to death, comes so far short
They might as well not try to go at all.
No, from the time when one is sick to death,
One is alone, and he dies more alone.

Friends make pretense of following to the grave,
But before one is in it, their minds are turned
And making the best of their way back to life
And living people, and things they understand.

But the world's evil. I won't have grief so
If I can change it. Oh, I won't, I won't!"

"There, you have said it all and you feel better.
You won't go now. You're crying. Close the door.
The heart's gone out of it: why keep it up.
Amy! There's someone coming down the road!"

"*You*—oh, you think the talk is all. I must go—
Somewhere out of this house. How can I make
   you—"
"If—you—do!" She was opening the door wider.
"Where do you mean to go? First tell me that.
I'll follow and bring you back by force. I *will!*—"

ROBERT FROST

THE CHILDHOOD

◆

DECLARATION OF INDEPENDENCE*

He will just do nothing at all.
He will just sit there in the noon-day sun.
And when they speak to him;—
he will not answer them
because he does not wish to
And when they tell him to eat his dinner
he will just laugh at them,
And he will not take his nap
Because he does not care to.
He will just sit there in the noon-day sun.
He will go away—and play with the panda,
and when they come to look for him,
he will stick them with spears
And put them in the garbage and put the cover on
And he will not go out in the fresh air
nor eat his vegetables
And he will grow thin as a marble
He will just do nothing at all.
He will just sit there in the noon-day sun.

WOLCOTT GIBBS

* Wolcott Gibbs heard this sung one evening by his four-year-old
son in the bathtub, and got the words printed in *The New Yorker*.
Celius Dougherty later set it to music.

DRAWING BY RONNIE C., GRADE ONE

For the sky, blue. But the six-year-
old searching his crayon-box, finds
no blue to match that sky
framed by the window—a see-through shine
over treetops, housetops. The wax colors
hold only dead light, not this water-flash
thinning to silver
at morning's far edge.
Gray won't do, either:
gray is for rain that you make with
dark slanting lines down-paper

                                        Try orange!

—Draw a large corner circle for sun, egg-yolk solid,
with yellow strokes, leaping outward
like fire bloom—a brightness shouting
flower-shape wind-shape joy-shape!

The boy sighs, with leg-twisting bliss creating . . .

It is done. The stubby crayons
(all ten of them) are stuffed back
bumpily into their box.

                                        RUTH LECHLITNER

MY PARENTS KEPT ME FROM CHILDREN WHO WERE ROUGH

My parents kept me from children who were rough
Who threw words like stones and who wore torn
   clothes.
Their thighs showed through rags. They ran in the
   street
And climbed cliffs and stripped by the country
   streams.

I feared more than tigers their muscles like iron
Their jerking hands and their knees tight on my
   arms.
I feared the salt-coarse pointing of those boys
Who copied my lisp behind me on the road.

They were lithe, they sprang out behind hedges
Like dogs to bark at my world. They threw mud
While I looked the other way, pretending to smile.
I longed to forgive them, but they never smiled.

STEPHEN SPENDER

BOY AT THE WINDOW

Seeing the snowman standing all alone
In dusk and cold is more than he can bear.
The small boy weeps to hear the wind prepare
A night of gnashings and enormous moan.
His tearful sight can hardly reach to where
The pale-faced figure with bitumen eyes
Returns him such a god-forsaken stare
As outcast Adam gave to Paradise.

The man of snow is, nonetheless, content,
Having no wish to go inside and die.
Still, he is moved to see the youngster cry.
Though frozen water is his element,
He melts enough to drop from one soft eye
A trickle of the purest rain, a tear
For the child at the bright pane surrounded by
Such warmth, such light, such love, and so much
    fear.

RICHARD WILBUR

THE BALLAD OF THE LIGHT-EYED
   LITTLE GIRL

Sweet Sally took a cardboard box,
And in went pigeon poor.
Whom she had starved to death but not
For lack of love, be sure.

The wind it harped as twenty men.
The wind it harped like hate.
It whipped our light-eyed little girl,
It made her wince and wait.

It screeched a hundred elegies
As it punished her light eyes
(Though only kindness covered these)
And it made her eyebrows rise.

"Now bury your bird," the wind it bawled,
"And bury him down and down
Who had to put his trust in one
So light-eyed and so brown."

"So light-eyed and so villainous,
Who whooped and who could hum
But could not find the time to toss
Confederate his crumb."

She has taken her passive pigeon poor
She has buried him down and down.
He never shall sally to Sally
Nor soil any roofs of the town.

She has sprinkled nail polish on dead dandelions.
And children have gathered around
Funeral for him whose epitaph
Is "Pigeon—Under the Ground."

GWENDOLYN BROOKS

THE BALLAD OF CHOCOLATE MABBIE

It was Mabbie without the grammar school gates.
And Mabbie was all of seven.
And Mabbie was cut from a chocolate bar.
And Mabbie thought life was heaven.

The grammar school gates were the pearly gates,
For Willie Boone went to school.
When she sat by him in history class
Was only her eyes were cool.

It was Mabbie without the grammar school gates
Waiting for Willie Boone.
Half hour after the closing bell!
He would surely be coming soon.

Oh, warm is the waiting for joys, my dears!
And it cannot be too long.
Oh, pity the little poor chocolate lips
That carry the bubble of song!

Out came the saucily bold Willie Boone.
It was woe for our Mabbie now.
He wore like a jewel a lemon-hued lynx
With sand-waves loving her brow.

It was Mabbie alone by the grammar school gates.
Yet chocolate companions had she:
Mabbie on Mabbie with hush in the heart.
Mabbie on Mabbie to be.

GWENDOLYN BROOKS

JANET WAKING

Beautifully Janet slept
Till it was deeply morning. She woke then
And thought about her dainty-feathered hen,
To see how it had kept.

One kiss she gave her mother.
Only a small one gave she to her daddy
Who would have kissed each curl of his shining
    baby;
No kiss at all for her brother.

"Old Chucky, old Chucky!" she cried,
Running across the world upon the grass
To Chucky's house, and listening. But alas,
Her Chucky had died.

It was a transmogrifying bee
Came droning down on Chucky's old bald head
And sat and put the poison. It scarcely bled,
But how exceedingly

And purply did the knot
Swell with the venom and communicate
Its rigor! Now the poor comb stood up straight
But Chucky did not.

So there was Janet
Kneeling on the wet grass, crying her brown hen
(Translated far beyond the daughters of men)
To rise and walk upon it.

And weeping fast as she had breath
Janet implored us, "Wake her from her sleep!"
And would not be instructed in how deep
Was the forgetful kingdom of death.

JOHN CROWE RANSOM

I am not yet born; O hear me.
  Let not the bloodsucking bat or the rat or the
  stoat or the club-footed ghoul come near me.

I am not yet born, console me.
I fear that the human race may with tall walls wall
  me, with strong drugs dope me, with wise lies
  lure me, on black racks rack me, in blood-baths
  roll me.

I am not yet born; provide me
With water to dandle me, grass to grow for me,
                     trees
  to talk to me, sky to sing to me, birds and a
                 white
    light in the back of my mind to guide me.

I am not yet born; forgive me
For the sins that in me the world shall commit, my
  words when they speak me, my thoughts when
    they think me, my treason engendered by
                traitors
    beyond me, my life when they murder by
      means of my hands, my death when they
      live me.

I am not yet born; rehearse me
In the parts I must play and the cues I must take
                    when
    old men lecture me, bureaucrats hector me,
        mountains frown at me, lovers laugh at me,
            the white waves call me to folly and the
                desert calls me to doom and the
                    beggar refuses my gift and my
                        children curse me.

I am not yet born; O hear me,
Let not the man who is beast or who thinks he is
    God come near me.

I am not yet born; O fill me
With strength against those who would freeze my
    humanity, would dragoon me into a lethal
        automaton, would make me a cog in a machine,
            a thing with one face, a thing, and against
                all those who would dissipate my entirety,
                    would blow me like thistledown hither
                        and thither or hither and thither
                            like water held in the
                                hands would spill me.

Let them not make me a stone and let them not
spill me. Otherwise kill me.

LOUIS MAC NEICE

ISOLATION

---◆---

PORTRAIT OF A GIRL WITH COMIC BOOK

Thirteen's no age at all. Thirteen is nothing.
It is not wit, or powder on the face,
Or Wednesday matinees, or misses' clothing,
Or intellect, or grace.
Twelve has its tribal customs. But thirteen
is neither boys in battered cars nor dolls,
Not *Sara Crewe* or movie magazine,
Or pennants on the walls.

Thirteen keeps diaries and tropical fish
(A month, at most); scorns jumpropes in the spring;
Could not, would fortune grant it, name its wish;
Wants nothing, everything;
Has secrets from itself, friends it despises;
Admits none of the terrors that it feels;
Owns a half a hundred masks but no disguises;
And walks upon its heels.

Thirteen's anomalous—not that, not this:
Not folded bud, or wave that laps a shore,
Or moth proverbial from the chrysalis.
Is the one age defeats the metaphor.
Is not a town, like childhood, strongly walled
But easily surrounded; is no city.
Nor, quitted once, can it be quite recalled—
Not even with pity.

PHYLLIS MC GINLEY

FIFTEEN

South of the bridge on Seventeenth
I found back of the willows one summer
day a motorcycle with engine running
as it lay on its side, ticking over
slowly in the high grass. I was fifteen.

I admired all that pulsing gleam, the
shiny flanks, the demure headlights
fringed where it lay; I led it gently
to the road and stood with that
companion, ready and friendly. I was fifteen.

We could find the end of a road, meet
the sky on out Seventeenth. I thought about
hills, and patting the handle got back a
confident opinion. On the bridge we indulged
a forward feeling, a tremble. I was fifteen.

Thinking, back farther in the grass I found
the owner, just coming to, where he had flipped
over the rail. He had blood on his hand, was pale—
I helped him walk to his machine. He ran his hand
over it, called me good man, roared away.

I stood there, fifteen.

WILLIAM STAFFORD

THE DREAMER

He spent his childhood hours in a den
of rushes, watching the gray rain braille
the surface of the river. Concealed
from the outside world, nestled within,
he was safe from parents, God, and eyes
that looked upon him accusingly,
as though to say: Even at your age,
you could do better. His camouflage
was scant, but it served, and at evening,
when fireflies burned holes into heaven,
he took the path homeward in the dark,
a small Noah, leaving his safe Ark.

WILLIAM CHILDRESS

THE CAVE

Sometimes when the boy was troubled he would go
    To a little cave of stone above the brook
And build a fire just big enough to glow
    Upon the ledge outside, then sit and look.
Below him was the winding silver trail
    Of water from the upland pasture springs,
And meadows where he heard the calling quail;
    Before him was the sky, and passing wings.

The tang of willow twigs he lighted there,
    Fragrance of meadows breathing slow and deep,
The cave's own musky coolness on the air,
    The scent of sunlight . . . all were his to keep.
We had such places—cave or tree or hill . . .
    And we are lucky if we keep them still.

GLENN W. DRESBACH

PREFACE TO A TWENTY VOLUME
   SUICIDE NOTE

Lately, I've become accustomed to the way
The ground opens up and envelops me
Each time I go out to walk the dog.
Or the broad edged silly music the wind
Makes when I run for a bus—

Things have come to that.

And now, each night I count the stars,
And each night I get the same number.
And when they will not come to be counted
I count the holes they leave.

Nobody sings anymore.

And then last night, I tiptoed up
To my daughter's room and heard her
Talking to someone, and when I opened
The door, there was no one there . . .
Only she on her knees,
Peeking into her own clasped hands.

                                        LEROI JONES

PASTORAL

When I was younger
it was plain to me
I must make something of myself.
Older now
I walk back streets
admiring the houses
of the very poor:
roof out of line with sides
the yards cluttered
with old chicken wire, ashes,
furniture gone wrong;
the fences and outhouses
built of barrel-staves
and parts of boxes, all,
if I am fortunate,
smeared a bluish green
that properly weathered
pleases me best
of all colors.

No one
will believe this
of vast import to the nation.

WILLIAM CARLOS WILLIAMS

IDENTITY

KENNEDY

I think that what he gave us most was pride.
It felt good to have a President like that:
bright, brave and funny and goodlooking.

I saw him once drive down East Seventy-second
    Street
in an open car, in the autumn sun
  (as he drove yesterday in Dallas).
His thatch of brown hair looked as though it had
    grown extra thick
the way our wood animals in Connecticut
grow extra fur for winter.
And he looked as though it was fun to be alive,
to be a politician,
to be President,
to be a Kennedy,
to be a man.

MOLLY KAZAN

YET DO I MARVEL

I doubt not God is good, well-meaning, kind,
And did He stoop to quibble could tell why
The little buried mole continues blind,
Why flesh that mirrors Him must some day die,
Make plain the reason tortured Tantalus
Is baited by the fickle fruit, declare
If merely brute caprice dooms Sisyphus
To struggle up a never-ending stair.
Inscrutable His ways are, and immune
To catechism by a mind too strewn
With petty cares to slightly understand
What awful brain compels His awful hand.
Yet do I marvel at this curious thing:
To make a poet black, and bid him sing!

COUNTEE CULLEN

THE NEGRO SPEAKS OF RIVERS

I've known rivers:
I've known rivers ancient as the world and older
than the flow of human blood in human veins.

My soul has grown deep like the rivers.

I bathed in the Euphrates when dawns were young.
I built my hut near the Congo and it lulled me to
sleep.
I looked upon the Nile and raised the pyramids
above it.
I heard the singing of the Mississippi when Abe
Lincoln went down to New Orleans, and I've
seen its muddy bosom turn all golden in the
sunset.

LANGSTON HUGHES

POWWOW*

They all see the same movies.
    They shuffle on one leg,
      Scuffing the dust up,
    Shuffle on the other.
They are all the same:
    A Sioux dance to the spirits,
    A war dance by four Chippewa,
    A Dakota dance for rain.
    We wonder why we came.
Even tricked out in the various braveries—
    Black buffalo tassels, beadwork, or the brilliant
    Feathers at the head, at the buttocks—
Even in long braids and the gaudy face paints,
    They all dance with their eyes turned
    Inward, like a woman nursing
A sick child she already knows
    Will die. For the time, she nurses it
    All the same. The loudspeakers shriek;
    We leave our bleacher seats to wander
    Among the wickiups and lean-tos
In a search for hot dogs. The Indians
    Are already packing; have
    Resumed green dungarees and khaki,
    Castoff combat issues of World War II.
    (Only the Iroquois do not come here;
They work in structural steel; they have a contract
    Building the United Nations
    And Air Force installations for our future
  wars.)

* Tama Reservation, Iowa, 1949.

These, though, have dismantled their hot-dog stand
      And have to drive all night
To jobs in truck stops and all-night filling stations.
      We ask directions and
   They scuttle away from us like moths.
      Past the trailers,
   Beyond us, one tepee is still shining
Over all the rest. Inside, circled by a ring
      Of children, in the glare
   Of one bare bulb, a shrunken fierce-eyed man
Squats at his drum, all bones and parchment,
      While his dry hands move
   On the drumhead, always drumming, always
Raising his toothless, drawn jaw to the light
   Like a young bird drinking, like a chained dog,
Howling his tribe's song for the restless young
      Who wander in and out.
      Words of such great age,
Not even he remembers what they mean.
      We tramp back to our car,
   Then nearly miss the highway, squinting
Through red and yellow splatterings on the
windshield,
   The garish and beautiful remains
      Of grasshoppers and dragonflies
That go with us, that do not live again.

W. D. SNODGRASS

FLORIDA ROAD WORKERS

I'm makin' a road
For the cars to fly by on,
Makin' a road
Through the palmetto thicket
For light and civilization
To travel on.

I'm makin' a road
For the rich to sweep over
In their big cars
And leave me standin' here.

Sure,
A road helps everybody!
Rich folks ride—
And I get to see 'em ride.

I ain't never seen nobody
Ride so fine before.
Hey, Buddy, Look!
I'm makin' a road!

LANGSTON HUGHES

PASTURES OF PLENTY

It's a mighty hard row that my poor hands has
  hoed,
My poor feet has traveled a hot dusty road;
Out of your Dust Bowl and westward we rolled,
And your deserts was hot and your mountains was
  cold.

I worked in your orchard of peaches and prunes,
Slept on the ground 'neath the light of the moon;
On the edge of your city you will see us and then,
We come with the dust and we go with the wind.

California, Arizona, I make all your crops,
Well, it's up north to Oregon to gather your hops;
Dig the beets from your ground, cut the grapes
  from your vine,
To set on your table your light, sparkling wine.

Green pastures of plenty from dry desert ground,
From the Grand Coulee Dam where the waters run
  down;
Every state in the union us migrants has been,
We'll work in this fight and we'll fight till we win.

It's always we rambled, that river and I,
All along your green valley I will work till I die;
My land I'll defend with my life if it be,
'Cause my pastures of plenty must always be free.

WOODY GUTHRIE

CALIBAN IN THE COAL MINES

God, we don't like to complain.
  We know that the mine is no lark.
But—there's the pools from the rain;
  But—there's the cold and the dark.

God, You don't know what it is—
  You, in Your well-lighted sky—
Watching the meteors whizz;
  Warm, with a sun always by.

God, if You had but the moon
  Stuck in Your cap for a lamp,
Even You'd tire of it soon,
  Down in the dark and the damp.

Nothing but blackness above
  And nothing that moves but the cars . . .
God, if You wish for our love,
  Fling us a handful of stars!

LOUIS UNTERMEYER

SUNDAY AFTERNOON

After the First Communion
and the banquet of mangoes and
bridal cake, the young daughters
of the coffee merchant lay down
for a long siesta, and their white dresses
lay beside them in quietness
and the white veils floated
in their dreams as the flies buzzed.
But as the afternoon
burned to a close they rose
and ran about the neighborhood
among the halfbuilt villas
alive, alive, kicking a basketball, wearing
other new dresses, of bloodred velvet.

DENISE LEVERTOV

TWO VOICES IN A MEADOW

A Milkweed

Anonymous as cherubs
Over the crib of God,
White seeds are floating
Out of my burst pod.
What power had I
Before I learned to yield?
Shatter me, great wind:
I shall possess the field.

A Stone

As casual as cow-dung
Under the crib of God,
I lie where chance would have me,
Up to the ears in sod.
Why should I move? To move
Befits a light desire.
The sill of Heaven would founder,
Did such as I aspire.

RICHARD WILBUR

GONE AWAY

When my body leaves me
I'm lonesome for it.
I've got

eyes, ears,
nose and mouth
and that's all.

Eyes
keep on seeing the
feather blue of the

cold sky,
mouth takes in
hot soup,
nose

smells the frost,

ears hear everything, all
the noises and absences,
but body

goes away to I don't know where
and it's lonesome to drift
above the space it
fills when it's here.

DENISE LEVERTOV

THE REBEL

When I
die
I'm sure
I will have a
Big Funeral . . .
Curiosity
seekers . . .
coming to see
if I
am really
Dead . . .
or just
trying to make
Trouble. . . .

MARI E. EVANS

REALITIES

BENDIX

This porthole overlooks a sea
Forever falling from the sky,
The water inextricably
Involved with buttons, suds, and dye.

Like bits of shrapnel, shards of foam
Fly heavenward; a bedsheet heaves,
A stocking wrestles with a comb,
And cotton angels wave their sleeves.

The boiling purgatorial tide
Revolves our dreary shorts and slips,
While Mother coolly bakes beside
Her little jugged apocalypse.

JOHN UPDIKE

AT BREAKFAST

Not quite
spherical
White
Oddly closed
and without a lid

A smooth miracle
here in my hand
Has it slid
from my sleeve?

The shape
of this box
keels me oval
Heels feel
its bottom
Nape knocks
its top

Seated
like a foetus
I look for
the dream-seam

What's inside?
A sun?
Off with its head
though it hasn't any
or is all head no body
a
One

Neatly
the knife scalps it
I scoop out
the braincap
soft
sweetly shuddering

Mooncream
this could be
Spoon
laps the larger
crescent
loosens a gilded
nucleus
from warm pap
A lyrical food

Opened
a seamless miracle
Ate a sun-germ
Good

MAY SWENSON

SONIC BOOM

I'm sitting in the living room,
When, up above, the Thump of Doom
Resounds. Relax. It's sonic boom.

The ceiling shudders at the clap,
The mirrors tilt, the rafters snap,
And Baby wakens from his nap.

"Hush, babe. Some pilot we equip,
Giving the speed of sound the slip,
Has cracked the air like a penny whip."

Our world is far from frightening; I
No longer strain to read the sky
Where moving fingers (jet planes) fly.
Our world seems much too tame to die.

And if it does, with one more pop,
I shan't look up to see it drop.

JOHN UPDIKE

                    ice cream
                    i scream
                    ice cream

        bright
        chosen   blurred
        lucent   rounded off
        sharp   made indefinite
                                            The side
        uneven   nubbled
        curving   the image   syrup-slow
        but willed   the transformation the taste
        jagged   glyceride
                        eating it   the memory
    silent   smirched
    magical, one   shimmering
    moment only   insatiable

        melting   accumulating,
                                            dribbling, about
        the shape itself   the cone   to drop
        the texture   cardboard
        a test   the surface
        an admission   sticky as plastic

        the recognition   immediate and
        deceiving the mind   unknown
        the lettering on the rim   trivial
        arguing sugar crystals,   enormous
        blatant, gummy, broken
                                    licked
        the patchwork grill   moist
        intensifying   still
        curving   firm

            outline   yet
            curling its   dis-
            fingers   appear-
            around,   ing
            and down

            possessing

            to draw, to take
            in the hand,
            to crunch
            its one
            point

                                    JONATHAN PRICE

[58]

THE BAT

By day the bat is cousin to the mouse.
He likes the attic of an aging house.

His fingers make a hat about his head.
His pulse beat is so slow we think him dead.

He loops in crazy figures half the night
Among the trees that face the corner light.

But when he brushes up against a screen,
We are afraid of what our eyes have seen:

For something is amiss or out of place
When mice with wings can wear a human face.

THEODORE ROETHKE

FOR A LAMB

I saw on the slant hill a putrid lamb,
Propped with daisies. The sleep looked deep,
The face nudged in the green pillow
But the guts were out for crows to eat.
Where's the lamb? whose tender plaint
Said all for the mute breezes.
Say he's in the wind somewhere,
Say, there's a lamb in the daisies.

RICHARD EBERHART

SUMMER: WEST SIDE

When on the coral-red steps of old brownstones
Puerto Rican boys, their white shirts luminous,
gather, and their laughter
conveys menace as far as Central Park West,

When the cheesecake shops on Broadway
keep open long into the dark,
and the Chinaman down in his hole of seven steps
leaves the door of his laundry ajar,
releasing a blue smell of starch,

When the indefatigable lines of parked cars
seem embedded in the tar,
and the swish of the cars on the Drive
seems urgently loud—

Then even the lapping of wavelets
on the boards of a barge on the Hudson
is audible,
and Downtown's foggy glow
fills your windows right up to the top.

And you walk in the mornings with your cool suit
sheathing the fresh tingle of your shower,
and the gratings idly steam,
and the damp path of the street-sweeper evapo-
    rates,

And—an oddly joyful sight—
the dentists' and chiropractors' white signs low
in the windows of the great ochre buildings on
    Eighty-sixth Street
Seem slightly darkened
by one more night's deposit of vigil.

JOHN UPDIKE

AUTO WRECK

Its quick soft silver bell beating, beating,
And down the dark one ruby flare
Pulsing out red light like an artery,
The ambulance at top speed floating down
Past beacons and illuminated clocks
Wings in a heavy curve, dips down,
And brakes speed, entering the crowd.
The doors leap open, emptying light;
Stretchers are laid out, the mangled lifted
And stowed into the little hospital.
Then the bell, breaking the hush, tolls once,
And the ambulance with its terrible cargo
Rocking, slightly rocking, moves away,
As the doors, an afterthought, are closed.

We are deranged, walking among the cops
Who sweep glass and are large and composed.
One is still making notes under the light.
One with a bucket douches ponds of blood
Into the street and gutter.
One hangs lanterns on the wrecks that cling,
Empty husks of locusts, to iron poles.

Our throats were tight as tourniquets,
Our feet were bound with splints, but now,
Like convalescents intimate and gauche,
We speak through sickly smiles and warn
With the stubborn saw of common sense,
The grim joke and the banal resolution.
The traffic moves around with care,
But we remain, touching a wound
That opens to our richest horror.

Already old, the question Who shall die?
Becomes unspoken Who is innocent?
For death in war is done by hands;
Suicide has cause and still birth, logic;
And cancer, simple as a flower, blooms.
But this invites the occult mind,
Cancels our physics with a sneer,
And spatters all we knew of denouement
Across the expedient and wicked stones.

KARL SHAPIRO

THE YACHTS

contend in a sea which the land partly encloses
shielding them from the too heavy blows
of an ungoverned ocean which when it chooses

tortures the biggest hulls, the best man knows
to pit against its beatings, and sinks them pitilessly.
Mothlike in mists, scintillant in the minute

brilliance of cloudless days, with broad bellying
    sails
they glide to the wind tossing green water
from their sharp prows while over them the crew
    crawls

ant like, solicitously grooming them, releasing,
making fast as they turn, lean far over and having
caught the wind again, side by side, head for the
    mark.

In a well guarded arena of open water surrounded
    by
lesser and greater craft which, sycophant,
    lumbering
and flittering follow them, they appear youthful,
    rare

as the light of a happy eye, live with the grace
of all that in the mind is feckless, free and
naturally to be desired. Now the sea which holds
    them
is moody, lapping their glossy sides, as if feeling

for some slightest flaw but fails completely.
Today no race. Then the wind comes again. The
  yachts

move, jockeying for a start, the signal is set and
  they
are off. Now the waves strike at them but they are
  too
well made, they slip through, though they take in
  canvas.

Arms with hands grasping seek to clutch at the
  prows.
Bodies thrown recklessly in the way are cut aside.
It is a sea of faces about them in agony, in despair

until the horror of the race dawns staggering the
  mind,
the whole sea become an entanglement of watery
  bodies
lost to the world bearing what they cannot hold.
  Broken,
beaten, desolate, reaching from the dead to be
  taken up
they cry out, failing, failing! their cries rising
in waves still as the skillful yachts pass over.

WILLIAM CARLOS WILLIAMS

CRYSTAL MOMENT

Once or twice this side of death
Things can make one hold his breath.

From my boyhood I remember
A crystal moment of September.

A wooded island rang with sounds
Of church bells in the throats of hounds.

A buck leaped out and took the tide
With jewels flowing past each side.

With his high head like a tree
He swam within a yard of me.

I saw the golden drop of light
In his eyes turned dark with fright.

I saw the forest's holiness
On him like a fierce caress.

Fear made him lovely past belief,
My heart was trembling like a leaf.

He leaned towards the land and life
With need above him like a knife.

In his wake the hot hounds churned,
They stretched their muzzles out and yearned.

They bayed no more, but swam and throbbed,
hunger drove them till they sobbed.

Pursued, pursuers reached the shore
And vanished. I saw nothing more.

So they passed, a pageant such
As only gods could witness much,

Life and death upon one tether
And running beautiful together.

ROBERT P. TRISTRAM COFFIN

TRAVELING THROUGH THE DARK

Traveling through the dark I found a deer
dead on the edge of the Wilson River road.
It is usually best to roll them into the canyon:
that road is narrow; to swerve might make more
    dead.

By glow of the tail-light I stumbled back of the car
and stood by the heap, a doe, a recent killing;
she had stiffened already, almost cold.
I dragged her off; she was large in the belly.

My fingers touching her side brought me the
    reason—
her side was warm; her fawn lay there waiting,
alive, still, never to be born.
Beside that mountain road I hesitated.

The car aimed ahead its lowered parking lights;
under the hood purred the steady engine.
I stood in the glare of the warm exhaust turning
    red;
around our group I could hear the wilderness
    listen.

I thought hard for us all—my only swerving—,
then pushed her over the edge into the river.

WILLIAM STAFFORD

ILLUSION

The pennycandystore beyond the El
is where I first
                    fell in love
                            with unreality
Jellybeans glowed in the semi-gloom
of that september afternoon
A cat upon the counter moved among
                                the licorice sticks
                    and tootsie rolls
      and Oh Boy Gum

Outside the leaves were falling as they died

A wind had blown away the sun

A girl ran in
Her hair was rainy
Her breasts were breathless in the little room
Outside the leaves were falling
                    and they cried
                            Too soon! too soon!

LAWRENCE FERLINGHETTI

EGO

When I was on Night Line,
flying my hands to park
a big-bird B-29,
I used to command the dark:
four engines were mine

to jazz; I was ground-crew,
an unfledged pfc,
but when I waved planes through
that flight line in Tennessee,
my yonder was wild blue.

Warming up, I was hot
on the throttle, logging an hour
of combat, I was the pilot
who rogered the tower.
I used to take off a lot.

With a flat-hat for furlough
and tin wings to sleep on,
I fueled my high-octane ego:
I buzzed, I landed my jeep on
the ramp, I flew low.

When a cross-country hop
let down, I was the big deal
who signaled big wheels to stop.
That's how I used to feel.
I used to get all revved up.

PHILIP BOOTH

LUCY IN THE SKY WITH DIAMONDS

Picture yourself in a boat on a river,
With tangerine trees and marmalade skies
Somebody calls you, you answer quite slowly,
A girl with kaleidoscope eyes.
Cellophane flowers of yellow and green,
Towering over your head.
Look for the girl with the sun in her eyes,
And she's gone.
Lucy in the sky with diamonds.
Follow her down to a bridge by a fountain
Where rocking horse people eat marshmallow pies,
Everyone smiles as you drift past the flowers,
That grow so incredibly high.
Newspaper taxis appear on the shore,
Waiting to take you away.
Climb in the back with your head in the clouds,
And you're gone.
Lucy in the sky with diamonds.
Picture yourself on a train in a station,
With plasticine porters with looking glass ties,
Suddenly someone is there at the turnstile,
The girl with the kaleidoscope eyes.

THE BEATLES

MUSEUMS

Museums offer us, running from among the 'buses,
A centrally heated refuge, parquet floors and
    sarcophaguses,
Into whose tall fake porches we hurry without a
    sound
Like a beetle under a brick that lies, useless on the
    ground.
Warmed and cajoled by the silence, the cowed
    cipher revives,
Mirrors himself in the cases of pots, paces himself
    by marble lives,
Makes believe it was he that was the glory that was
    Rome,
Soft on his cheek the nimbus of other people's
    martyrdom,
And then returns to the street, his mind an arena
    where sprawls
Any number of consumptive Keatses and dying
    Gauls.

LOUIS MAC NEICE

SUBURBAN MADRIGAL

Sitting here in my house,
looking through my windows
diagonally at my neighbor's house,
I see his sun-porch windows;
they are filled with blue-green,
the blue-green of my car,
which I parked in front of my house,
more or less, up the street,
where I can't directly see it.

How promiscuous is
the world of appearances!
How frail are property laws!
To him his window is filled with his
things: his lamp, his plants, his radio.
How annoyed he would be to know
that my car, legally parked,
yet violates his windows,
paints them full
(to me) of myself, my car,
my well-insured '55 Fordor Ford
a gorgeous green sunset streaking his panes.

JOHN UPDIKE

SAND HILL ROAD

The landscape here is Africa
in California, scattered stands
of flattened Eucalyptus spread
their shallow horizontal hands
and make a spotted shade for leopards
or giraffes. I look for leopards
under every tree, for lions
in the grass; the passage signs
are not the tracks of elephants
but panting yellow tractors, stamping
down the bushes, trampling on
the slender trees, like elephants.

But still, the river draws a belt
of green across the brown, the veldt
is still a perfect veldt. I know
that if at dusk I climb a tree
and if the moon is bright, I could
be watching when the cautious,
softly snorting herd of bulldozers
comes watering at night.

MORTON GROSSER

THE BIG ROCK CANDY MOUNTAINS

One evenin' as the sun went down
And the jungle fire was burnin',
Down the track came a hobo hikin'
And he said: "Boys, I'm not turnin',
I'm headed fer a land that's far away
Beside the crystal fountains,
So come with me, we'll all go see
The Big Rock Candy Mountains."

In the Big Rock Candy Mountains,
There's a land that's fair and bright,
Where the handouts grow on bushes,
And you sleep out every night.
Where the boxcars are all empty,
And the sun shines every day
On the birds and the bees and the cigarette trees,
And the lemonade springs where the bluebird
    sings,
In the Big Rock Candy Mountains.

In the Big Rock Candy Mountains,
All the cops have wooden legs,
The bulldogs all have rubber teeth,
And the hens lay soft-boiled eggs.
The farmers' trees are full of fruit,
And the barns are full of hay.
Oh, I'm bound to go where there ain't no snow,
Where the rain don't pour, the wind don't blow,
In the Big Rock Candy Mountains.

In the Big Rock Candy Mountains,
You never change your socks,
And the little streams of alcohol
Come tricklin' down the rocks.
There the brakemen have to tip their hats
And the railroad bulls are blind.
There's a lake of stew and of whisky too,
You can paddle all around 'em in a big canoe,
In the Big Rock Candy Mountains.

In the Big Rock Candy Mountains,
All the jails are made of tin,
And you can bust right out again
As soon as you are in.
There ain't no short-handled shovels,
No axes, saws or picks.
I'm going to stay where you sleep all day,
Where they hung the Turk that invented work,
In the Big Rock Candy Mountains.

ANONYMOUS

THE LIFEGUARD

In a stable of boats I lie still,
From all sleeping children hidden.
The leap of a fish from its shadow
Makes the whole lake instantly tremble.
With my foot on the water, I feel
The moon outside.

Take the utmost of its power.
I rise and go out through the boats.
I set my broad sole upon silver,
On the skin of the sky, on the moonlight,
Stepping outward from earth onto water
In quest of the miracle.

This village of children believed
That I could perform as I dived
For one who had sunk from my sight.
I saw his cropped haircut go under.
I leapt, and my steep body flashed
Once, in the sun.

Dark drew all the light from my eyes.
Like a man who explores his death
By the pull of his slow-moving shoulders,
I hung head down in the cold,
Wide-eyed, contained, and alone
Among the weeds,

And my fingertips turned into stone
From clutching immovable blackness.
Time after time I leapt upward

Exploding in breath, and fell back
From the change in the children's faces
At my defeat.

Beneath them, I swam to the boathouse
With only my life in my arms
To wait for the lake to shine back
At the risen moon with such power
That my steps on the light of the ripples
Might be sustained.

Beneath me is nothing but brightness
Like the ghost of a snow field in summer.
As I move toward the center of the lake,
Which is also the center of the moon,
I am thinking of how I may be
The savior of one

Who has already died in my care.
The dark trees fade from around me.
The moon's dust hovers together.
I call softly out, and the child's
Voice answers through blinding water.
Patiently, slowly,

He rises, dilating to break
The surface of stone with his forehead.
He is one I do not remember
Having ever seen in his life.
The ground that I stand on is trembling
Upon his smile.

I wash the black mud from my hands.
On a light given off by the grave,
I kneel in the quick of the moon
At the heart of a distant forest
And hold in my arms a child
Of water, water, water.

JAMES DICKEY

DISSENT

SKETCH FROM LOSS OF MEMORY

On Sundays I ran my mare past
the church, leaned to her camber
at Georgetown Corner throwing
sparks from the cobbled curve.
"Never run your horse on macadam,
or shoot the minister in the heart
of his sermon with a hoofbeat,"
they told me.

           The neighbor's boy
shines his motorcycles in the evenings.
"A bum in boots," they call him.
I say: "Better boots than burned ankles."
The wet days, I spent soaping
my tack until the unguent oozed
from the pores of leather,
and two weeks braiding a quirt
from four strands of rawhide.

         The boy leans
at a windy corner, horsepower roaring
between his legs with a smell of burnt grease
as sweet as horse sweat. I like him,
on Sunday rousing us with his revved engine
from our dreams of potato pudding;
his mettle pulls my memory up
big as the noon over the barn roof.

SONYA DORMAN

SHE'S LEAVING HOME

Wednesday morning at five o'clock as
the day begins
Silently closing her bedroom door
Leaving the note that she hoped would
say more
She goes downstairs to the kitchen
clutching her handkerchief
Quietly turning the backdoor key
Stepping outside she is free.
She (We gave her most of our lives)
is leaving (Sacrificed most of our lives)
home (We gave her everything
       money could buy)
She's leaving home after living alone
For so many years, Bye, Bye
Father snores as his wife gets into her
dressing gown
Picks up the letter that's lying there
Standing alone at the top of the stairs
She breaks down and cries to her husband
Daddy our baby's gone.

Why would she treat us so thoughtlessly
How could she do this to me.
She (We never thought of ourselves)
is leaving (Never a thought for ourselves)
home (We struggled hard all
              our lives to get by)
She's leaving home after living alone
For so many years. Bye, Bye
Friday morning at nine o'clock she is far
away
Waiting to keep the appointment she
made
Meeting a man from the motor trade.
She (What did we do that was wrong)
is having (We didn't know it was wrong)
fun (Fun is the one thing that
            money can't buy)
Something inside that was always denied
For so many years. Bye, Bye
She's leaving home bye bye.

THE BEATLES

SOUTHBOUND ON THE FREEWAY

A tourist came in from Orbitville,
parked in the air, and said:

The creatures of this star
are made of metal and glass.

Through the transparent parts
you can see their guts.

Their feet are round and roll
on diagrams—or long

measuring tapes—dark
with white lines.

They have four eyes.
The two in the back are red.

Sometimes you can see a 5-eyed
one, with a red eye turning

on the top of his head.
He must be special—

the others respect him,
and go slow,

when he passes, winding
among them from behind.

They all hiss as they glide,
like inches, down the marked

tapes. Those soft shapes,
shadowy inside

the hard bodies—are they
their guts or their brains?

MAY SWENSON

LITTLE BOXES

Little boxes on the hillside,
Little boxes made of ticky tacky little boxes little
    boxes,
Little boxes all the same.
There's a green one and a pink one and a blue one
    and a yellow one,
And they're all made out of ticky tacky
    and they all look just the same.

And the people in the houses all went to the
    University
Where they were put in boxes, little boxes, all the
    same.
And there's doctors and there's lawyers and there's
    business executives
And they're all made out of ticky tacky and they all
    look just the same.

And they all play on the golf course
    and drink their martini dry
And they all have pretty children and the children
    go to school
And the children go to summer camp and then to
    the University
Where they all get put in boxes and they all come
    out the same.

And the boys go into business and marry and raise
    a family
In boxes, little boxes, little boxes all the same.

There's a green one and a pink one and a blue one
and a yellow one
And they're all made out of ticky tacky and they all
look just the same.

MALVINA REYNOLDS

TARGET

The moon holds nothing in her arms;
  She is as empty as a drum.
She is a cipher, though she charms;
  She is delectable but dumb.
She has no factories or farms,
Or men to sound the fire-alarms
  When the marauding missiles come.

We have no cause to spare that face
  Suspended fatly in the sky.
She does not help the human race.
  Surely, she shines when bats flit by
And burglars seek their burgling-place
And lovers in a soft embrace
  Among the whispering bushes lie—

But that is all. Dogs still will bark
  When cottage doors are lightly knocked,
And poachers crawl about the park
  Cursing the glint on guns halfcocked;
None of the creatures of the dark
Will, in their self-absorption, mark
  That visage growing slightly pocked.

R. P. LISTER

"next to of course god america i
love you land of the pilgrims' and so forth oh
say can you see by the dawn's early my
country 'tis of centuries come and go
and are no more what of it we should worry
in every language even deafanddumb
thy sons acclaim your glorious name by gorry
by jingo by gee by gosh by gum
why talk of beauty what could be more beautiful than these heroic happy dead
who rushed like lions to the roaring slaughter
they did not stop to think they died instead
then shall the voice of liberty be mute?"

He spoke. And drank rapidly a glass of water

e. e. cummings

VAPOR TRAIL REFLECTED IN THE FROG
  POND

1

The old watch: their
thick eyes
puff and foreclose by the moon. The young, heads
trailed by the beginnings of necks,
shiver,
in the guarantee they shall be bodies.

In the frog pond
the vapor trail of a SAC bomber creeps,

I hear its drone, drifting, high up
in immaculate ozone.

2

And I hear,
coming over the hills, America singing,
her varied carols I hear:
crack of deputies' rifles practicing their aim on stray
  dogs at night,
sput of cattleprod,
TV groaning at the smells of the human body,
curses of the soldier as he poisons, burns, grinds,
  and stabs
the rice of the world,
with open mouth, crying strong, hysterical curses.

And by rice paddies in Asia
bones
wearing a few shadows
walk down a dirt road, smashed
bloodsuckers on their heel, knowing
the flesh a man throws down in the sunshine
dogs shall eat
and the flesh that is upthrown in the air
shall be seized by birds,
shoulder blades smooth, unmarked by old feather-
   holes,
hands rivered
by blue, erratic wanderings of the blood,
eyes crinkled up
as they gaze up at the drifting sun that gives us our
   lives,
seed dazzled over the footbattered blaze of the
   earth.

GALWAY KINNELL

THE BODY POLITIC

I shot my friend to save my country's life.
After the happy bullet struck him dead,
I was saluted by the drum and fife
Corps of a high school while the traitor bled.

I understood the duty they assigned
And shot my friend to save my sanity:
Keeping disorder from the state of mind
Was mental hygiene as it seemed to me.

I never thought until I pulled the trigger
But that I did the difficult and good:
I thought republics stood for something bigger,
For the mind of man, as Plato said they stood.

Talkative Socrates committed treason
Against instinct and natural emotion
By drinking hemlock on behalf of reason.
Too late I learn: A nation's just a notion.

DONALD HALL

pity this busy monster,manunkind,

not. Progress is a comfortable disease:
your victim (death and life safely beyond)

plays with the bigness of his littleness
—electrons deify one razorblade
into a mountainrange;lenses extend

unwish through curving wherewhen till unwish
returns on its unself.

A world of made
is not a world of born—pity poor flesh

and trees,poor stars and stones,but never this
fine specimen of hypermagical

ultraomnipotence.   We doctors know
a hopeless case if—listen:there's a hell
of a good universe next door;let's go

e. e. cummings

THE UNKNOWN CITIZEN

(To JS/07/M/378 This Marble Monument
Is Erected by the State)

He was found by the Bureau of Statistics to be
One against whom there was no official complaint,
And all the reports on his conduct agree
That, in the modern sense of an old-fashioned
    word, he was a saint.
For in everything he did he served the Greater
    Community.
Except for the War till the day he retired
He worked in a factory and never got fired,
But satisfied his employers, Fudge Motors Inc.
Yet he wasn't a scab or odd in his views,
For his Union reports that he paid his dues,
(Our report on his Union shows it was sound)
And our Social Psychology workers found
That he was popular with his mates and liked a
    drink.
The Press are convinced that he bought a paper
    every day
And that his reactions to advertisements were
    normal in every way.
Policies taken out in his name prove that he was
    fully insured,
And his Health-card shows he was once in hospital
    but left it cured.
Both Producers Research and High-Grade Living
    declare
He was fully sensible to the advantages of the
    Installment Plan

And had everything necessary to the Modern Man,
A phonograph, a radio, a car and a frigidaire.
Our researchers into Public Opinion are content
That he held the proper opinion for the time of
  year;
When there was peace, he was for peace; when
  there was war, he went.
He was married and added five children to the
  population,
Which our Eugenist says was the right number for
  a parent of his generation,
And our teachers report that he never interfered
  with their education.
Was he free? Was he happy? The question is
  absurd:
Had anything been wrong, we should certainly have
  heard.

W. H. AUDEN

THE ANGRY MAN

The other day I chanced to meet
An angry man upon the street—
A man of wrath, a man of war,
A man who truculently bore
Over his shoulder, like a lance,
A banner labeled "Tolerance."

And when I asked him why he strode
Thus scowling down the human road,
Scowling, he answered, "I am he
Who champions total liberty—
Intolerance being, ma'am, a state
No tolerant man can tolerate.

"When I meet rogues," he cried, "who choose
To cherish oppositional views,
Lady, like this, and in this manner,
I lay about me with my banner
Till they cry mercy, ma'am." His blows
Rained proudly on prospective foes.

Fearful, I turned and left him there
Still muttering, as he thrashed the air,
"Let the Intolerant beware!"

PHYLLIS MC GINLEY

COMMUNICATION

SIREN SONG

This is the one song everyone
would like to learn: the song
that is irresistible:

the song that forces men
to leap overboard in squadrons
even though they see the beached skulls

the song nobody knows
because anyone who has heard it
is dead, and the others can't remember.

Shall I tell you the secret
and if I do, will you get me
out of this bird suit?

I don't enjoy it here
squatting on this island
looking picturesque and mythical.

with these two feathery maniacs,
I don't enjoy singing
this trio, fatal and valuable.

I will tell the secret to you,
to you, only to you.
Come closer. This song

is a cry for help: Help me!
Only you, only you can,
you are unique

at last. Alas
it is a boring song
but it works every time.

MARGARET ATWOOD

THOUGHTS WHILE DRIVING HOME

Was I clever enough? Was I charming?
  Did I make at least one good pun?
Was I disconcerting? Disarming?
  Was I wise? Was I wan? Was I fun?

  Did I answer that girl with white shoulders
  Correctly, or should I have said
  (Engagingly), "Kierkegaard smolders,
  But Eliot's ashes are dead"?

  And did I, while being a smarty,
  Yet some wry reserve slyly keep,
  So they murmured, when I'd left the party,
  "He's deep. He's deep. He's deep"?

                                        JOHN UPDIKE

CONFESSION OVERHEARD IN A SUBWAY

You will ask how I came to be eavesdropping, in
   the first place.
The answer is, I was not.
The man who confessed to these several crimes
   (call him John Doe) spoke into my right ear on a
   crowded subway train, while the man whom he
   addressed (call him Richard Roe) stood at my
   left. Thus, I stood between them, and they
   talked, or sometimes shouted, quite literally
   straight through me.
How could I help but overhear?
Perhaps I might have moved away to some other
   strap. But the aisles were full.
Besides, I felt, for some reason, curious.

"I do not deny my guilt," said John Doe. "My own,
   first, and after that my guilty knowledge of still
   further guilt.
I have counterfeited often, and successfully.
I have been guilty of ignorance, and talking with
   conviction. Of intolerable wisdom, and keeping
   silent.

Through carelessness, or cowardice, I have short-
   ened the lives of better men. And the name for
   that is murder.
All my life I have been a receiver of stolen goods."

"Personally, I always mind my own business," said
   Richard Roe. "Sensible people don't get into
   those scrapes."

I was not the only one who overheard this confession.

Several businessmen, bound for home, and housewives and mechanics, were within easy earshot.

A policeman sitting in front of us did not lift his eyes, at the mention of murder, from his paper.

Why should I be the one to report these crimes?

You will understand why this letter to your paper is anonymous. I will sign it: Public-spirited Citizen, and hope that it cannot be traced.

KENNETH FEARING

AN ECHO:
SONNET TO AN EMPTY PAGE

Voice: Echo:

How from emptiness can I make a start?   Start
And starting, must I master joy or grief?   Grief
But is there consolation in the heart?   Art
O cold reprieve, where's natural relief?   Leaf
Leaf blooms, burns red before delighted eyes. Dies
Her beauty makes of dying, ecstasy.   See
Yet what's the end of our life's long disease?   Ease
If death is not, who is my enemy?   Me
Then are you glad that I must end in sleep?   Leap
I'd leap into the dark if dark were true.   True
And in that night would you rejoice or weep? Weep
What contradiction makes you take this view? You
I feel your calling leads me where I go,   Go
But whether happiness is there, you know.   No.

ROBERT PACK

LONELINESS

I was about to go, and said so;
And I had almost started for the door.
But he was all alone in the sugar-house,
And more lonely than he'd ever been before.
We'd talked for half an hour, almost,
About the price of sugar, and how I like my school,
And he had made me drink some syrup hot,
Telling me it was better that way than when cool.

And I agreed, and thanked him for it,
And said good-bye, and was about to go.
Want to see where I was born?
He asked me quickly. How to say no?

The sugar-house looked over miles of valley.
He pointed with a sticky finger to a patch of snow
Where he was born. The house, he said, was gone.
I can understand these people better, now I know.

BROOKS JENKINS

HOW SHE RESOLVED TO ACT

"I shall be careful to say nothing at all
About myself or what I know of him
Or the vaguest thought I have—no matter how dim,
Tonight if it so happen that he call."

And not ten minutes later the doorbell rang
And into the hall he stepped as he always did
With a face and a bearing that quite poorly hid
His brain that burned and his heart that fairly sang
And his tongue that wanted to be rid of the truth.

As well as she could, for she was very loath
To signify how she felt, she kept very still,
But soon her heart cracked loud as a coffee mill
And her brain swung like a comet in the dark
And her tongue raced like a squirrel in the park.

MERRILL MOORE

A RITUAL TO READ TO EACH OTHER

If you don't know the kind of person I am
and I don't know the kind of person you are
a pattern that others made may prevail in the world
and following the wrong god home we may miss
    our star.

For there is many a small betrayal in the mind
a shrug that lets the fragile sequence break
sending with shouts the horrible errors of
    childhood
storming out to play through the broken dyke.

And as elephants parade holding each elephant's
    tail,
but if one wanders the circus won't find the park,
I call it cruel and maybe the root of all cruelty
to know what occurs but not recognize the fact.

And so I appeal to a voice, to something shadowy,
a remote important region in all who talk:
though we could fool each other, we should
    consider—
lest the parade of our mutual life get lost in the
    dark.

For it is important that awake people be awake,
or a breaking line may discourage them back to
    sleep;
the signals we give—yes or no, maybe—
should be clear: the darkness around us is deep.

WILLIAM STAFFORD

GRANDMOTHER, ROCKING

Last night I dreamed of an old lover,
I had not seen him in forty years.
When I awoke,
I saw him on the street:
his hair was white,
his back stooped.
How could I say hello?
He would have been puzzled all day
about who the young girl was
who smiled at him.
So I let him go on his way.

                            EVE MERRIAM

LOVE

---◆---

FOR ANNE

With Annie gone,
Whose eyes to compare
With the morning sun?

Not that I did compare,
But I do compare
Now that she's gone.

SONG

I almost went to bed
without remembering
the four white violets
I put in the button-hole
of your green sweater

and how I kissed you then
and you kissed me
shy as though I'd
never been your lover.

LEONARD COHEN

      To be in love
Is to touch things with a lighter hand.

In yourself you stretch, you are well.
You look at things
Through his eyes.
            A Cardinal is red.
            A sky is blue.
Suddenly you know he knows too.
He is not there but
You know you are tasting together
The winter, or light spring weather.

His hand to take your hand is overmuch.
Too much to bear.

You cannot look in his eyes
Because your pulse must not say
What must not be said.

When he
Shuts a door—
Is not there—
Your arms are water.

And you are free
With a ghastly freedom.

You are the beautiful half
Of a golden hurt.

You remember and covet his mouth,
To touch, to whisper on.

Oh when to declare
Is certain Death!

Oh when to apprize
Is to mesmerize,

To see fall down, the Column of Gold,
Into the commonest ash.

GWENDOLYN BROOKS

SONNET

Some for a little while do love, and some for long;
And some rare few forever and for aye;
Some for the measure of a poet's song,
And some the ribbon width of a summer's day.
Some on a golden crucifix do swear,
And some in blood do plight a fickle troth;
Some struck divinely mad may only stare,
And out of silence weave an iron oath.

So many ways love has none may appear
The bitter best, and none the sweetest worst;
Strange food the hungry have been known to bear,
And brackish water slakes an utter thirst.
It is a rare and tantalizing fruit
Our hands reach for, but nothing absolute.

COUNTEE CULLEN

PLACES, LOVED ONES

No, I have never found
The place where I could say
This is my proper ground,
Here I shall stay;
Nor met that special one
Who has an instant claim
On everything I own
Down to my name;
To find such seems to prove
You want no choice in where
To build, or whom to love;
You ask them to bear
You off irrevocably,
So that it's not your fault
Should the town turn dreary,
The girl a dolt.

Yet, having missed them, you're
Bound, none the less, to act
As if what you settled for
Mashed you, in fact;
And wiser to keep away
From thinking you still might trace
Uncalled-for to this day
Your person, your place.

PHILIP LARKIN

somewhere i have never travelled,gladly beyond
any experience,your eyes have their silence:
in your most frail gesture are things which enclose
    me,
or which i cannot touch because they are too near

your slightest look easily will unclose me
though i have closed myself as fingers,
you open always petal by petal myself as Spring
    opens
(touching skilfully,mysteriously)her first rose

or if your wish be to close me,i and
my life will shut very beautifully,suddenly,
as when the heart of this flower imagines
the snow carefully everywhere descending;

nothing which we are to perceive in this world
    equals
the power of your intense fragility:whose texture
compels me with the colour of its countries,
rendering death and forever with each breathing

(i do not know what it is about you that closes
and opens;only something in me understands
the voice of your eyes is deeper than all roses)
nobody,not even the rain,has such small hands

                    e. e. cummings

FOR HETTIE

My wife is left-handed,
Which implies a fierce de-
termination. A complete other
worldliness. IT"S WIERD BABY
The way some folks
are always trying to be different.
A sin and a shame.

But then, she's been a bohemian
all her life . . . black stockings,
refusing to take orders. I sit
patiently, trying to tell her
what's right. TAKE THAT DAMM
PENCIL OUTTA THAT HAND. YOU'RE
RITING BACKWARDS and such. But,
to no avail. And it shows
in her work. Left-handed coffee,
left-handed eggs: when she comes
in at night . . . it's her left hand
offered for me to kiss. DAMM.

And now her belly droops over the seat.
They say it's a child. But
I ain't quite so sure.

LEROI JONES

THE RIVER-MERCHANT'S WIFE: A LETTER

While my hair was still cut straight across my fore-
 head
I played about the front gate, pulling flowers.
You came by on bamboo stilts, playing horse,
You walked about my seat, playing with blue plums.
And we went on living in the village of Chokan:
Two small people, without dislike or suspicion.

At fourteen I married My Lord you.
I never laughed, being bashful.
Lowering my head, I looked at the wall.
Called to, a thousand times, I never looked back.

At fifteen I stopped scowling,
I desired my dust to be mingled with yours
Forever and forever and forever.
Why should I climb the look out?

At sixteen you departed,
You went into far Ku-to-yen, by the river of swirling
   eddies,
And you have been gone five months.
The monkeys make sorrowful noise overhead.

You dragged your feet when you went out.
By the gate now, the moss is grown, the different
   mosses,
Too deep to clear them away!
The leaves fall early this autumn, in wind.
The paired butterflies are already yellow with
   August
Over the grass in the West garden;
They hurt me. I grow older.
If you are coming down through the narrows of the
   river Kiang,
Please let me know beforehand,
And I will come out to meet you
As far as Cho-fu-sa.

RIHAKU*

* *Rihaku:* the Japanese name for Li Po, the Chinese poet (705–762).
Ezra Pound reconstructed several poems by Li Po.

TO D—, DEAD BY HER OWN HAND

My dear, I wonder if before the end
You ever thought about a children's game—
I'm sure you must have played it too—in which
You ran along a narrow garden wall
Pretending it to be a mountain ledge
So steep a snowy darkness fell away
On either side to deeps invisible;
And when you felt your balance being lost
You jumped because you feared to fall, and thought
For only an instant: that was when I died.

That was a life ago. And now you've gone,
Who would no longer play the grown-ups' game
Where, balanced on the ledge above the dark,
You go on running and you don't look down,
Nor ever jump because you fear to fall.

HOWARD NEMEROV

WAR

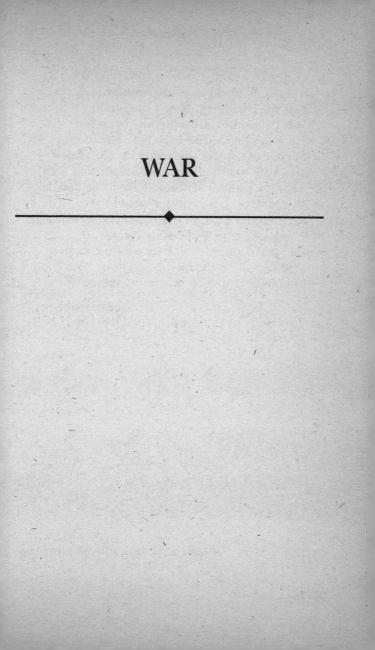

THE SONNET-BALLAD*

O mother, mother, where is happiness?
They took my lover's tallness off to war.
Left me lamenting. Now I cannot guess
What I can use an empty heart-cup for.
He won't be coming back here any more.
Some day the war will end, but, oh, I knew
When he went walking grandly out that door
That my sweet love would have to be untrue.
Would have to be untrue. Would have to court
Coquettish death, whose impudent and strange
Possessive arms and beauty (of a sort)
Can make a hard man hesitate—and change.
And he will be the one to stammer, "Yes."
Oh mother, mother, where is happiness?

GWENDOLYN BROOKS

* Number 3 from "Appendix to the Anniad" leaves from a loose-leaf war diary.

Where have all the flowers gone,
Long time passing?
Where have all the flowers gone,
Long time ago?
Where have all the flowers gone?
The girls have picked them every one.
Oh, when will you ever learn?
Oh, when will you ever learn?

Where have all the young girls gone,
Long time passing?
Where have all the young girls gone,
Long time ago?
Where have all the young girls gone?
They've taken husbands every one.
Oh, when will you ever learn?
Oh, when will you ever learn?

Where have all the young men gone,
Long time passing?
Where have all the young men gone,
Long time ago?
Where have all the young men gone?
They're all in uniform.
Oh, when will we ever learn?
Oh, when will we ever learn?

Where have all the soldiers gone,
Long time passing?
Where have all the soldiers gone,
Long time ago?

Where have all the soldiers gone?
They've gone to graveyards, every one.
Oh, when will they ever learn?
Oh, when will they ever learn?

Where have all the graveyards gone,
Long time passing?
Where have all the graveyards gone,
Long time ago?
Where have all the graveyards gone?
They're covered with flowers every one.
Oh, when will they ever learn?
Oh, when will they ever learn?

Where have all the flowers gone,
Long time passing?
Where have all the flowers gone,
Long time ago?
Where have all the flowers gone?
Young girls picked them every one.
Oh, when will they ever learn?
Oh, when will they ever learn?

PETE SEEGER

NAMING OF PARTS

To-day we have naming of parts. Yesterday,
We had daily cleaning. And to-morrow morning,
We shall have what to do after firing. But to-day,
To-day we have naming of parts. Japonica
Glistens like coral in all of the neighbouring
    gardens,
    And to-day we have naming of parts.

This is the lower sling swivel. And this
Is the upper sling swivel, whose use you will see,
When you are given your slings. And this is the
    piling swivel,
Which in your case you have not got. The branches
Hold in the gardens their silent, eloquent gestures,
    Which in our case we have not got.

This is the safety-catch, which is always released
With an easy flick of the thumb. And please do not
    let me
See anyone using his finger. You can do it quite
    easy
If you have any strength in your thumb. The
    blossoms
Are fragile and motionless, never letting anyone see
    Any of them using their finger.

And this you can see is the bolt. The purpose of
    this
Is to open the breech, as you see. We can slide it
Rapidly backwards and forwards: we call this
Easing the spring. And rapidly backwards and
    forwards
The early bees are assaulting and fumbling the
    flowers:
    They call it easing the Spring.

They call it easing the Spring: it is perfectly easy
If you have any strength in your thumb: like the
    bolt,
And the breech, and the cocking-piece, and the
    point of balance,
Which in our case we have not got; and the
    almond-blossom
Silent in all of the gardens and the bees going
    backwards and forwards,
    For to-day we have naming of parts.

HENRY REED

OF BOMBS AND BOYS

Among boy-crawling bamboo
the slowburn fuse
ignites

a greenflow serpent hisses
whips
        coils
                strikes
        recoils
fangs deepsunk
in a fortune cookie

the jungle blossoms
a starspangled second

        scatter of fireworms

the ember Deep Hurt glows
in the no sound

                    RICHARD CORBIN

my sweet old etcetera
aunt lucy during the recent

war could and what
is more did tell you just
what everybody was fighting

for,
my sister

isabel created hundreds
 (and
hundreds) of socks not to
mention shirts fleaproof earwarmers

etcetera wristers etcetera, my
mother hoped that

i would die etcetera
bravely of course my father used
to become hoarse talking about how it was
a privilege and if only he
could meanwhile my
self etcetera lay quietly
in the deep mud et

cetera
 (dreaming,
et

        cetera, of
Your smile
eyes knees and of your Etcetera)

                              e. e. cummings

THE DEATH OF THE BALL TURRET
GUNNER

From my mother's sleep I fell into the State,
And I hunched in its belly till my wet fur froze.
Six miles from earth, loosed from its dream of life,
I woke to black flak and the nightmare fighters.
When I died they washed me out of the turret with
  a hose.

RANDALL JARRELL

AN IRISH AIRMAN FORESEES HIS DEATH

I know that I shall meet my fate
Somewhere among the clouds above;
Those that I fight I do not hate,
Those that I guard I do not love;
My country is Kiltartan Cross,
My countrymen Kiltartan's poor,
No likely end could bring them loss
Or leave them happier than before.
Nor law, nor duty bade me fight,
Nor public men, nor cheering crowds,
A lonely impulse of delight
Drive to this tumult in the clouds;
I balanced all, brought all to mind,
The years to come seemed waste of breath,
A waste of breath the years behind
In balance with this life, this death.

WILLIAM BUTLER YEATS

ULTIMA RATIO REGUM

The guns spell money's ultimate reason
In letters of lead on the Spring hillside.
But the boy lying dead under the olive trees
Was too young and too silly
To have been notable to their important eye.
He was a better target for a kiss.

When he lived, tall factory hooters never
  summoned him.
Nor did restaurant plate-glass doors revolve to
  wave him in.
The world maintained its traditional wall
Round the dead with their gold sunk deep as a
  well,
Whilst his life, intangible as a Stock Exchange
  rumor, drifted outside.

O too lightly he threw down his cap
One day when the breeze threw petals from the
  trees.
The unflowering wall sprouted with guns,
Machine-gun anger quickly scythed the grasses.
Flags and leaves fell from hands and branches;
The tweed cap rotted in the nettles.

Consider his life which was valueless
In terms of employment, hotel ledgers, news files.
Consider. One bullet in ten thousand kills a man.
Ask. Was so much expenditure justified
On the death of one so young, and so silly
Lying under the olive trees, O world, O death?

STEPHEN SPENDER

THE CONSCIENTIOUS OBJECTOR

The gates clanged and they walked you into jail
More tense than felons but relieved to find
The hostile world shut out, the flags that dripped
From every mother's windowpane, obscene
The bloodlust sweating from the public heart,
The dog authority slavering at your throat.
A sense of quiet, of pulling down the blind
Possessed you. Punishment you felt was clean.

The decks, the catwalks, and the narrow light
Composed a ship. This was a mutinous crew
Troubling the captains for plain decencies,
A Mayflower brim with pilgrims headed out
To establish new theocracies to west,
A Noah's ark coasting the topmost seas
Ten miles above the sodomites and fish.
These inmates loved the only living doves.

Like all men hunted from the world you made
A good community, voyaging the storm
To no safe Plymouth or green Ararat;
Trouble or calm, the men with Bibles prayed,
The gaunt politicals construed our hate.
The opposite of all armies, you were best
Opposing uniformity and yourselves;
Prison and personality were your fate.

You suffered not so physically but knew
Maltreatment, hunger, ennui of the mind.
Well might the soldier kissing the hot beach
Erupting in his face damn all your kind.
Yet you who saved neither yourselves nor us
Are equally with those who shed the blood
The heroes of our cause. Your conscience is
What we come back to in the armistice.

KARL SHAPIRO

I'VE GOT TO KNOW

Why do your warships sail on my waters?
Why do your bombs drop down from my sky?
Why do you burn my towns and my cities?
I want to know, friend, I want to know why!

Chorus: I've got to know, friend, I've got to know!
Hungry lips ask me wherever I go!
Comrades and friends all falling around me,
I've got to know, friend, I've got to know.

Why do these boats haul death to my people?
Nitro explosives, cannons and guns?
Where is my food, my soap and my warm clothes?
I've got to know, friend, I've got to know. (Chorus)

You keep me in jail and you lock me in prison.
Your hospital's jammed, and your asylum is full.
What made your cop kill my trade union worker?
I've got to know, friend, I've got to know! (Chorus)

Why do these warships sail on my ocean?
Why do these bombs drop down from my sky?
Why doesn't your ship bring some food and some
  clothing?
I've got to know, friend, I've got to know why.
  (Chorus)

WOODY GUTHRIE

PAIN

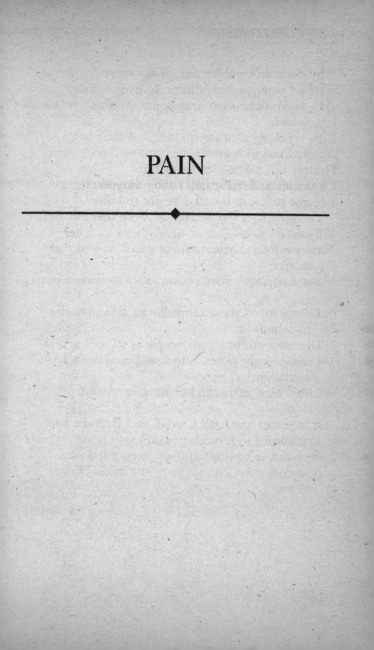

THE HEROES

I dreamed of war-heroes, of wounded war-heroes
With just enough of their charms shot away
To make them more handsome. The women moved
  nearer
To touch their brave wounds and their hair
  streaked with gray.

I saw them in long ranks ascending the gang-
  planks;
The girls with the doughnuts were cheerful and
  gay.
They minded their manners and muttered their
  thanks;
The Chaplain advised them to watch and to pray.

They shipped these rapscallions, these sea-sick
  battalions
To a patriotic and picturesque spot;
They gave them new bibles and marksmen's
  medallions,
Compasses, maps, and committed the lot.

A fine dust has settled on all that scrap metal.
The heroes were packaged and sent home in parts
To pluck at a poppy and sew on a petal
And count the long night by the strike of their
  hearts.

LOUIS SIMPSON

SURGICAL WARD

They are and suffer; that is all they do;
A bandage hides the place where each is living,
His knowledge of the world restricted to
The treatment that the instruments are giving.

And lie apart like epochs from each other
—Truth in their sense is how much they can bear;
It is not talk like ours, but groans they smother—
And are remote as plants; we stand elsewhere.

For who when healthy can become a foot?
Even a scratch we can't recall when cured,
But are boist'rous in a moment and believe

In the common world of the uninjured, and cannot
Imagine isolation. Only happiness is shared,
And anger, and the idea of love.

W. H. AUDEN

HUNCHBACK GIRL: SHE THINKS OF HEAVEN

My Father, it is surely a blue place
And straight. Right. Regular. Where I shall find
No need for scholarly nonchalance or looks
A little to the left or guards upon the
Heart to halt love that runs without crookedness
Along its crooked corridors. My Father,
It is a planned place surely. Out of coils,
Unscrewed, released, no more to be marvelous,
I shall walk straightly through most proper halls
Proper myself, princess of properness.

GWENDOLYN BROOKS

DARK GIRL

Easy on your drums,
Easy wind and rain,
And softer on your horns,
She will not dance again.

Come easy little leaves
Without a ghost of sound
From the China trees
To the fallow ground.

Easy, easy drums
And sweet leaves overhead,
Easy wind and rain;
Your dancing girl is dead.

ARNA BONTEMPS

IT'S HERE IN THE

Here in the newspaper—the wreck of the East
   Bound.
A photograph bound to bring on cardiac asthenia.
There is a blur that mists the page!
On one side is a gloom of dreadful harsh.
Then breaks flash lights up sheer.
There is much huge about. I suppose then
         those no's are people
     between that suffering of—.
     (what more have we? for Christ's sake, no!)
Something of a full stop of it
crash of blood and the still shock
     of stark sticks and an immense swift gloss,
And two dead no's lie aghast still.
One casts a crazed eye and the other's
Closed dull.
     the heap up twists
         such
as to harden the unhard and unhard
the hardened.

                                        RUSSELL ATKINS

HURT HAWKS

The broken pillar of the wing jags from the clotted
    shoulder,
The wing trails like a banner in defeat,
No more to use the sky forever but live with famine
And pain a few days: cat nor coyote
Will shorten the week of waiting for death, there is
    game without talons.
He stands under the oak-bush and waits
The lame feet of salvation; at night he remembers
    freedom
And flies in a dream, the dawns ruin it.

He is strong and pain is worse to the strong,
    incapacity is worse.
The curs of the day come and torment him
At distance, no one but death the redeemer will
    humble that head,
The intrepid readiness, the terrible eyes.
The wild God of the world is sometimes merciful to
    those
That ask mercy, not often to the arrogant.
You do not know him, you communal people, or
    you have forgotten him;
Intemperate and savage, the hawk remembers him;
Beautiful and wild, the hawks, and men that are
    dying, remember him.

I'd sooner, except the penalties, kill a man than a
    hawk; but the great redtail
Had nothing left but unable misery

From the bone too shattered for mending, the wing
    that trailed under his talons when he moved.
We had fed him six weeks, I gave him freedom,
He wandered over the foreland hill and returned in
    the evening, asking for death,
Not like a beggar, still eyed with the old
Implacable arrogance. I gave him the lead gift in
    the twilight. What fell was relaxed,
Owl-downy, soft feminine feathers; but what
Soared: the fierce rush: the night-herons by the
    flooded river cried fear at its rising
Before it was quite unsheathed from reality.

ROBINSON JEFFERS

RECOLLECTIONS

SONNET TO MY MOTHER

Most near, most dear, most loved and most far,
Under the window where I often found her
Sitting as huge as Asia, seismic with laughter,
Gin and chicken helpless in her Irish hand,
Irresistible as Rabelais but most tender for
The lame dogs and hurt birds that surround her,—
She is a procession no one can follow after
But be like a little dog following a brass band.

She will not glance up at the bomber or
    condescend
To drop her gin and scuttle to a cellar,
But lean on the mahogany table like a mountain
Whom only faith can move, and so I send
O all my faith and all my love to tell her
That she will move from mourning into morning.

GEORGE BARKER

Fortune
        has its cookies to give out
which is a good thing

           since it's been a long time since

     that summer in Brooklyn
when they closed off the street
     one hot day
       and the

                FIREMEN

        turned on their hoses

and all the kids ran out in it

    in the middle of the street

and there were

       maybe a couple dozen of us

                   out there

with the water squirting up

      to the

      sky

                    and all over
                        us

    there was maybe only six of us
                                kids altogether
        running around in our
                            barefeet and birthday
        suits
        and I remember Molly but then
    the firemen stopped squirting their hoses
        all of a sudden and went
                back in
            their firehouse
                and
    started playing pinochle again
        just as if nothing
            had ever
                    happened
    while I remember Molly
            looked at me and
    ran in
    because I guess really we were the only ones there

                            LAWRENCE FERLINGHETTI

AUNT HELEN

Miss Helen Slingsby was my maiden aunt,
And lived in a small house near a fashionable
　square
Cared for by servants to the number of four.
Now when she died there was silence in heaven
And silence at her end of the street.
The shutters were drawn and the undertaker wiped
　his feet—
He was aware that this sort of thing had occurred
　before.
The dogs were handsomely provided for,
But shortly afterwards the parrot died too.
The Dresden clock continued ticking on the
　mantelpiece,
And the footman sat upon the dining-table
Holding the second housemaid on his knees—
Who had always been so careful while her mistress
　lived.

T. S. ELIOT

BELLS FOR JOHN WHITESIDE'S DAUGHTER

There was such speed in her little body,
And such lightness in her footfall,
It is no wonder her brown study
Astonishes us all.

Her wars were bruited in our high window.
We looked among orchard trees and beyond,
Where she took arms against her shadow,
Or harried unto the pond

The lazy geese, like a snow cloud
Dripping their snow on the green grass,
Tricking and stopping, sleepy and proud,
Who cried in goose, Alas,

For the tireless heart within the little
Lady with rod that made them rise
From their noon apple-dreams and scuttle
Goose-fashion under the skies!

But now go the bells, and we are ready,
In one house we are sternly stopped
To say we are vexed at her brown study,
Lying so primly propped.

JOHN CROWE RANSOM

ELEGY FOR JANE
(My student, thrown by a horse)

I remember the neckcurls, limp and damp as ten-
   drils;
And her quick look, a sidelong pickerel smile;
And how, once startled into talk, the light syllables
   leaped for her,
And she balanced in the delight of her thought,
A wren, happy, tail into the wind,
Her song trembling the twigs and small branches.
The shade sang with her;
The leaves, their whispers turned to kissing;
And the mold sang in the bleached valleys under
   the rose.

Oh, when she was sad, she cast herself down into
   such a pure depth,
Even a father could not find her:
Scraping her cheek against straw;
Stirring the clearest water.

My sparrow, you are not here,
Waiting like a fern, making a spiny shadow.
The sides of wet stones cannot console me,
Nor the moss, wound with the last light.

If only I could nudge you from this sleep,
My maimed darling, my skittery pigeon.
Over this damp grave I speak the words of my love:
I, with no rights in this matter,
Neither father nor lover.

                              THEODORE ROETHKE

[153]

THE ELEMENTARY SCENE

Looking back in my mind I can see
The white sun like a tin plate
Over the wooden turning of the weeds;
The street jerking—a wet swing—
To end by the wall the children sang.

The thin grass by the girls' door,
Trodden on, straggling, yellow and rotten,
And the gaunt field with its one tied cow—
The dead land waking sadly to my life—
Stir, and curl deeper in the eyes of time.

The rotting pumpkin under the stairs
Bundled with switches and the cold ashes
Still holds for me, in its unwavering eyes,
The stinking shapes of cranes and witches,
Their path slanting down the pumpkin's sky.

Its stars beckon through the frost like cottages
(Homes of the Bear, the Hunter—of that absent
  star,
The dark where the flushed child struggles into
  sleep)
Till, leaning a lifetime to the comforter,
I float above the small limbs like their dream:

I, I, the future that mends everything.

RANDALL JARRELL

Now as I was young and easy under the apple
  boughs
About the lilting house and happy as the grass was
  green,
    The night above the dingle starry,
        Time let me hail and climb
    Golden in the heydays of his eyes,
And honored among wagons I was prince of the
  apple towns
And once below a time I lordly had the trees and
  leaves
        Trail with daisies and barley
    Down the rivers of the windfall light.

And as I was green and carefree, famous among the
  barns
About the happy yard and singing as the farm was
  home,
    In the sun that is young once only,
        Time let me play and be
    Golden in the mercy of his means,
And green and golden I was huntsman and herds-
  man, the calves
Sang to my horn, the foxes on the hills barked
  clear and cold,
        And the sabbath rang slowly
In the pebbles of the holy streams.

All the sun long it was running, it was lovely, the
    hay
Fields high as the house, the tunes from the chim-
    neys, it was air
        And playing, lovely and watery
            And fire green as grass.
        And nightly under the simple stars
As I rode to sleep the owls were bearing the farm
    away,
All the moon long I heard, blessed among stables,
    the night-jars
        Flying with the ricks, and the horses
            Flashing into the dark.

And then to awake, and the farm, like a wanderer
    white
With the dew, come back, the cock on his shoulder:
    it was all
        Shining, it was Adam and maiden,
            The sky gathered again
        And the sun grew round that very day.
So it must have been after the birth of the simple
    light
In the first, spinning place, the spellbound horses
    walking warm
        Out of the whinnying green stable
            On to the fields of praise.

And honored among foxes and pheasants by the
    gay house
Under the new made clouds and happy as the heart
    was long,

In the sun born over and over,
  I ran my heedless ways,
My wishes raced through the house high hay
And nothing I cared, at my sky blue trades, that
  time allows
In all his tuneful turning so few and such morning
  songs
    Before the children green and golden
      Follow him out of grace,

Nothing I cared, in the lamb white days, that time
  would take me
Up to the swallow thronged loft by the shadow of
  my hand,
    In the moon that is always rising,
      Nor that riding to sleep
    I should hear him fly with the high fields
And wake to the farm forever fled from the child-
  less land.
Oh as I was young and easy in the mercy of his
  means,
      Time held me green and dying
    Though I sang in my chains like the sea.

DYLAN THOMAS

ACKNOWLEDGMENTS

"Little Brand New Baby (For Andrew Arthur Okun, Born September 29, 1962)," words and music by Tom Paxton: © copyright 1962, 1965 by Cherry Lane Music, Inc. Used by permission. All rights reserved.

"The Name" by Robert Creeley: copyright © 1961 by Robert Creeley. Reprinted with the permission of Charles Scribner's Sons, an imprint of Macmillan Publishing Company, from *For Love: Poems 1950–1960* by Robert Creeley. Copyright © 1962 by Robert Creeley.

"Taught Me Purple" by Evelyn Tooley Hunt: published in *Negro Digest*, February 1964. Reprinted by permission of the author.

"Mother to Son" by Langston Hughes: copyright 1926 by Alfred A. Knopf, Inc., and renewed 1954 by Langston Hughes. Reprinted from *Selected Poems* by Langston Hughes. Reprinted by permission of Alfred A. Knopf, Inc., a subsidiary of Random House, Inc.

"That Dark Other Mountain" by Robert Francis: reprinted with the permission of Robert Francis and the University of Massachusetts Press from *Come Out into the Sun: Poems New and Selected*. Copyright by Robert Francis.

"What Shall He Tell That Son?" by Carl Sandburg: from *The People, Yes* by Carl Sandburg. Copyright 1936 by Harcourt, Brace & World, Inc.; renewed 1964 by Carl Sandburg. Reprinted by permission of Harcourt Brace Jovanovich, Inc.

"My Papa's Waltz" by Theodore Roethke: copyright 1942 by Hearst Magazine, Inc. From the book *The Collected Poems of Theodore Roethke*. Reprinted by permission of Doubleday & Company, Inc., a division of Bantam Doubleday Dell Publishing Group, Inc.

"The Empty Woman" by Gwendolyn Brooks: from *Blacks* by Gwendolyn Brooks, copyright 1987 by Gwendolyn Brooks. Published by The David Company, P.O. Box 19355, Chicago, Illinois 60619. Reprinted by permission of the author.

"Stark Boughs on the Family Tree" by Mary Oliver: © 1968 by The New York Times Company and reprinted by permission. Copyright © 1968 by Mary Oliver and used by permission.

INDEX OF FIRST LINES

A father sees a son nearing manhood. 9

After the First Communion 48

Among boy-crawling bamboo 131

Anonymous as cherubs 49

As casual as cow-dung 49

A tourist came in from Orbitville, 87

Beautifully Janet slept 27

Be natural, 3

By day the bat is cousin to the mouse. 59

contend in a sea which the land partly encloses 65

Easy on your drums, 143

For the sky, blue. But the six-year- 21

Fortune 149

From my mother's sleep I fell into the State, 134

God, we don't like to complain. 47

Here in the newspaper— the wreck of the East Bound. 144

He saw her from the bottom of the stairs 14

He spent his childhood hours in a den 34

He was found by the Bureau of Statistics to be 97

He will just do nothing at all. 20

Hey, Little Brand New Baby, 2

How from emptiness can I make a start? 107

I almost went to bed 114

I am not yet born; O hear me. 29

ice cream 58

I doubt not God is good, well-meaning, kind, 41

I dreamed of war-heroes, of wounded war-heroes 140

If you don't know the kind of person I am 110

I know that I shall meet my fate 134

I'm makin' a road 45

I'm sitting in the living room, 57

In a stable of boats I lie still, 80

I remember the neckcurls, limp and damp as tendrils; 153

I saw on the slant hill a putrid lamb, 60

"I shall be careful to say nothing at all 109

I shot my friend to save my country's life, 95

I think that what he gave us most was pride. 40

It's a mighty hard row that my poor hands has hoed, 46

Its quick soft silver bell beating, beating, 63

It was Mabbie without the grammar school gates. 26

I've known rivers: 42

I was about to go, and said so; 108

Last night I dreamed of an old lover, 111

Lately, I've become accustomed to the way 36

Little boxes on the hillside, 89

Looking back in my mind I can see 154

Miss Helen Slingsby was my maiden aunt, 151

Most near, most dear, most loved and most far, 148

Museums offer us, running from among the 'buses, 75

My dear, I wonder if before the end 123

My father could go down a mountain faster than I 7

My Father, it is surely a blue place 142

My father was the first to hear 8

My mother taught me purple 5

My parents kept me from children who were rough 22

my sweet old etcetera 132

My wife is left-handed, 120

"next to of course god america i 92

No, I have never found 118

Not quite 55

Now as I was young and easy under the apple boughs 155

O mother, mother, where is happiness? 126

Once or twice this side of death 67

One evenin' as the sun went down 78

On Sundays I ran my mare past 84

Picture yourself in a boat on a river, 74

pity this busy monster,manunkind, 96

Seeing the snowman standing all alone 23

Sitting here in my house, 76

Some for a little while do love, and some for long; 117

Sometimes when the boy was troubled he would go 35

somewhere i have never travelled, gladly beyond 119

South of the bridge on Seventeenth 33

Sweet Sally took a cardboard box, 24

The broken pillar of the wing jags from the clotted shoulder, 145

The empty woman took toys! 12

The gates clanged and they walked you into jail 136

The guns spell money's ultimate reason 135

The landscape here is Africa 77

The moon holds nothing in her arms; 91

The old watch: their 93

The other day I chanced to meet 99

The pennycandystore beyond the El 72

There was such speed in her little body, 152

The whiskey on your breath 11

They all see the same movies. 43

They are and suffer; that is all they do; 141

Thirteen's no age at all. Thirteen is nothing. 32

This is the one song everyone would like to learn: 102

This porthole overlooks a sea 54

To be in love 115

To-day we have naming of parts. Yesterday, 129

Traveling through the dark I found a deer 69

Up in the attic on row on row, 13

Was I clever enough? Was I charming? 104

Wednesday morning at five o'clock as 85

Well, Son, I'll tell you 6

When I 51

When I was on Night Line, 73

When I was younger 37

When my body leaves me 50

When on the coral-red steps of old brownstones 61

Where have all the flowers
    gone, 127
While my hair was still cut
    straight across my
    forehead 121
Why do your warships sail
    on my waters? 138

With Annie gone, 114

You will ask how I came to
    be eavesdropping, in
    the first place. 105

INDEX OF AUTHORS
AND TITLES

The Angry Man 99
Anonymous 78
At Breakfast 55
Atkins, Russell 144
Atwood, Margaret, 102
Auden, W. H. 97, 141
Aunt Helen 151
Auto Wreck 63

*The Ballad of Chocolate
    Mabbie* 26
*The Ballad of the Light-Eyed
    Little Girl* 24
Barker, George 148
The Bat 59
The Beatles, 74, 85
*Bells for John Whiteside's
    Daughter* 152
Bendix 54
*The Big Rock Candy
    Mountains* 78
The Body Politic 95
Bontemps, Arna 143
Booth, Philip 73
Boy at the Window 23
Brooks, Gwendolyn 12, 24,
    26, 115, 126, 142

Caliban in the Coal Mines 47
The Cave 35

Childress, William 34
Coffin, Robert P. Tristram
    67
Cohen, Leonard 114
*Confession Overheard in a
    Subway* 105
The Conscientious Objector
    136
Corbin, Richard 131
Creeley, Robert 3
Crystal Moment 67
Cullen, Countee 41, 117
cummings, e. e. 92, 96,
    119, 132

*To D—, Dead by Her Own
    Hand* 123
Dark Girl 143
*The Death of the Ball Turret
    Gunner* 134
*Declaration of
    Independence* 20
Dickey, James 80
Dorman, Sonya 84
*Drawing by Ronnie C., Grade
    One* 21
The Dreamer 34
Dresbach, Glenn W. 35

Eberhart, Richard 60
An Echo: Sonnet to an Empty Page, 107
Ego 73
Elegy for Jane 153
The Elementary Scene 154
Eliot, T. S. 151
The Empty Woman 12
Evans, Mari E. 51

Fearing, Kenneth 105
Ferlinghetti, Lawrence 72, 149
Fern Hill 155
Fifteen 33
Florida Road Workers 45
For Anne 114
For Hettie 120
For a Lamb 60
Francis, Robert 7
Frost, Robert 14

The Geese 8
Gibbs, Wolcott 20
Gone Away 50
Grandmother, Rocking, 111
Grosser, Morton 77
Guthrie, Woody 46, 138

Hall, Donald 95
The Heroes 140
Home Burial 14
How She Resolved to Act 109
Hughes, Langston 6, 42, 45
Hunchback Girl: She Thinks of Heaven 142
Hunt, Evelyn Tooley 5
Hurt Hawks 145

Ice Cream 58
An Irish Airman Foresees His Death 134
It's Here In The 144
I've Got To Know 138

Janet Waking 27
Jarrell, Randall 134, 154
Jeffers, Robinson 145
Jenkins, Brooks 108
Jones, LeRoi 36, 120

Kazan, Molly 40
Kennedy 40
Kinnell, Galway 93

Larkin, Philip 118
Lechlitner, Ruth 21
Levertov, Denise 48, 50
The Lifeguard 80
Lister, R. P. 91
Little Boxes 89
Little Brand New Baby 2
Loneliness 108
Lucy in the Sky with Diamonds 74

MacNeice, Louis 29, 75
McGinley, Phyllis 32, 99
Merriam Eve, 111
Moore, Merrill 109
Mother to Son 6
Museums 75
My Papa's Waltz 11
My Parents Kept Me from Children Who Were Rough 22
my sweet old etcetera 132

The Name 3
Naming of Parts 129

The Negro Speaks of Rivers 42
Neuverov, Howard, 123
next to of course god america i 92
Number 7 149
Number 20 72

Of Bombs and Boys 131
Oliver, Mary 13

Pack, Robert 107
Pastoral 37
Pastures of Plenty 46
Paxton, Tom 2
Peck, Richard 8
pity this busy monster,manunkind 96
Places, Loved Ones 118
Portrait of a Girl with Comic Book 32
Powwow 43
Prayer Before Birth 29
Preface to a Twenty Volume Suicide Note 36
Price, Jonathan 58

Ransom, John Crowe 27, 152
The Rebel 51
Reed, Henry 129
Reynolds, Malvina 89
Rihaku 121
A Ritual To Read to Each Other 110
The River-Merchant's Wife: A Letter 121
Roethke, Theodore 11, 59, 153

Sandburg, Carl 9
Sand Hill Road 77

Seeger, Pete 127
Shapiro, Karl 63, 136
She's Leaving Home 85
Simpson, Louis 140
Siren Song 102
Sketch from Loss of Memory 84
Snodgrass, W. D. 43
somewhere i have never travelled 119
Song 114
Sonic Boom 57
Sonnet 117
The Sonnet-Ballad 126
Sonnet to My Mother 148
Southbound on the Freeway 87
Spender, Stephen 22, 135
Stafford, William 33, 69, 110
Stark Boughs on the Family Tree 13
Suburban Madrigal 76
Summer: West Side 61
Sunday Afternoon 48
Surgical Ward 141
Swenson, May 55, 87

Target 91
Taught Me Purple 5
That Dark Other Mountain 7
Thomas, Dylan 155
Thoughts While Driving Home 104
To Be in Love 115
Traveling Through the Dark 69
Two Voices in a Meadow 49

Ultima Ratio Regum 135
The Unknown Citizen 97

Untermeyer, Louis 47
Updike, John 54, 57, 61, 76, 104

Vapor Trail Reflected in the Frog Pond 93

What Shall He Tell That Son? 9

Where Have All the Flowers Gone? 127
Wilbur, Richard 23, 49
Williams, William Carlos 37, 65

The Yachts 65
Yeats, William Butler 134
Yet Do I Marvel 41